...y and
British Politics
1902–1951

Stuart Ball

LONGMAN
London and New York

Longman Group Limited,
Longman House, Burnt Mill, Harlow,
Essex CM20 2JE, England
and Associated Companies throughout the world.

Published in the United States of America
by Longman Inc., New York.

First published 1995

Set in 10/11 point Baskerville (Linotron)
Produced through Longman Malaysia, PA

ISBN 0 582 08002 9

British Library Cataloguing in Publication Data
Ball, Stuart
   Conservative Party and British Politics,
   1902–51. — (Seminar Studies in History)
   I. Title II. Series
   324.2410409

   ISBN 0–582–08002–9

Library of Congress Cataloging-in-Publication Data
Ball, Stuart, 1956–
      The Conservative Party and British politics, 1902–1951/Stuart Ball.
         p.   cm. — (Seminar studies in history)
      Includes bibliographical references and index.
      ISBN 0–582–08002–9: £4.99
      1. Conservative Party (Great Britain) —History—20th century.
   2. Great Britain—Politics and government—20th century. I. Title.
   II. Series.
   JN1129.C7B27   1995
   324.24104'0904—dc20   94–31525
                                                           CIP

Contents

Contents

Seminar Studies in History

Introduction

Seminar Studies in History offer clearly written, authoritative and stimulating introductions to important topics. They cover major themes in British and European history.

The authors are acknowledged experts in their field and the books are works of scholarship in their own right as well as providing a survey of current historical interpretations. They are regularly updated to take account of the latest research.

The material is carefully selected to give the reader sufficient confidence to handle different aspects of the theme as well as being enjoyable and interesting to read.

Seminar Studies in History were the creation of Patrick Richardson, a gifted and original teacher who died tragically in an accident in 1979. The continuing vitality of the series is a tribute to his vision.

Structure of the Book

Each title has a brief introduction or background to the subject, a substantial section of analysis, followed by an assessment, a selection of documents which enable the reader to see how historical judgements are reached and to question and challenge them, a glossary which explains key terms, and a bibliography which provides a guide to further reading.

Throughout the book references are made to the Bibliography, to the relevant document within the Documents section (Part 4), and to definitions in the Glossary. These are indicated as follows:

- **Bibliography** – a bold number in round brackets (**6**) in the text refers to the corresponding entry in the Bibliography
- **Document** – a bold number in square brackets, preceded by 'doc.' [**doc. 4**] refers to the document in

the Documents section which relates to/illuminates the passage/idea

Roger Lockyer

The General Editor

Roger Lockyer, Emeritus Reader in History at the University of London, is the author of a number of books on Tudor and Stuart history including *Buckingham*, a political biography of George Villiers, first Duke of Buckingham, 1592–1628, and *The Early Stuarts: A Political History of England, 1603–1642*. He has also written two widely used general surveys – *Tudor and Stuart Britain* and *Habsburg and Bourbon Europe*.

The Author

Stuart Ball is lecturer in History at the University of Leicester. He is author of *Baldwin and the Conservative Party: The Crisis of 1929–31* (Yale University Press, 1988) and co-editor of *Conservative Century: The Conservative Party since 1900* (Oxford University Press, 1994).

Acknowledgements

Conservative Party Archive Poster No. 35 ("Let the Lighthouse of Conservatism save SS Britain from the Rocks of Socialism", 1929). The Bodleian Library, Oxford.

Foreword

The Conservative Party has been the dominant force in British politics during the last hundred years: either alone or as the main element in a coalition, it has governed for almost seventy of them. Since 1900 its opponents have been able to depend upon a secure majority in only three parliaments: the Liberals in 1906–10, Labour in 1945–50 and 1966–70. On the other hand, no Conservative ministry has lacked a working majority in the House of Commons, even if in 1951 and 1992 it was only a narrow one. Despite this remarkable record of success, the Conservatives were for many years the Cinderella of British political history. The familiar and the constant are apt to be overlooked, and, like the poor, the Conservative Party seems always to have been with us. From the early 1950s to the late 1970s the rise of Labour and the decline of the Liberals attracted much greater interest, due partly to the drama involved in the convulsion on the left and partly to the sympathies and assumptions of the day. The expansion of higher education and the opening of many modern archives coincided with the one period during which Labour could credibly be regarded as the natural party of government, the decade and a half from 1964 to 1979. A final factor contributed to the general neglect: whilst few still subscribed uncritically to the jibe that the Conservatives were the 'stupid' party, there was and still is an unspoken assumption that they are the simple party. In fact, in doctrine, ethos and methods of business they are the most complex and subtle of the main political groups. Assumptions which are based upon taking the particular forms of the left-of-centre parties as the only proper norm are especially inappropriate: much more is going on within the Conservative Party than is often apparent on the surface, and the unwritten rules are more important than the written ones (7).

Biographies have been a particular feature of historical writing on the modern history of the Conservative Party. The most important are those of the party leaders Bonar Law (20) and Baldwin (45), which appeared in 1955 and 1969 respectively; in between, studies of other key figures such as Joseph Chamberlain (19),

Derby (**26**) and Milner (**33**) filled out the picture and printed many private documents. Broader questions began to be addressed in the 1970s with the publication of several general surveys (**2, 3, 8**). The most elegant of these appeared at the beginning of the decade with the first edition of Lord Blake's wide-ranging Ford Lectures, *The Conservative Party from Peel to Churchill* (**1**); the most authoritative appeared at the end in the form of John Ramsden's lucid *The Age of Balfour and Baldwin 1902–40* (**6**).

Since the mid-1970s an increasing stream of more detailed studies in monograph and particularly in article form has augmented the steady flow of biographies. This heightened level of interest was encouraged by two parallel developments. The first of these was the range of primary sources which became available during the 1970s, culminating in the opening of the Conservative Party Archive at the Bodleian Library, Oxford. Secondly, the party's controversial period in office under Margaret Thatcher from 1979 to 1990 and its continued electoral success stimulated questions about the nature and history of the most adaptable, enduring and effective right-of-centre party in the world. As a result, since 1979 the history of Conservatism has attracted increasing attention from younger scholars. However, the history of the Conservative Party since 1900 has not been covered in any consistent depth. It is revealing that the period of faction and failure in the Edwardian years has attracted by far the most attention, principally focused upon the strife caused by tariff reform and the constitutional crises of 1909–14. Apart from the events surrounding the fall of the Lloyd George coalition in 1922, the long period of Conservative success between the wars has been less fully explored. The even greater dearth on the years after 1940 is partly due to the fact that the key sources are only now becoming accessible; apart from the authorised biographies (**34, 35, 38**), there is only an early though perceptive study of the recovery in opposition in 1945–51 (**161**) and a handful of recent articles.

Although unevenly, the boundaries of understanding and analysis have advanced considerably since the last general histories of the party were published in the 1970s. This has led to a new synthesis, *Conservative Century* (**7**), which investigates key themes in its history from 1900 to the early 1990s. Seminar Studies can only follow the wider trend. Although the volume on the rise of Labour was published in 1972 and that on the decline of the Liberals in 1981, only now can the picture be completed with a parallel assessment of the role of the Conservatives in our recent political history.

Note on Nomenclature

From 1886 until after the First World War the key issue in politics was the Irish question, and in recognition of both their stance on this issue and their alliance with the Liberal Unionists, the Conservative Party was known as the 'Unionist Party' or 'the Unionists' from the 1890s to the early 1920s. The contemporary usage is followed in this book, and the label 'Unionist' is used as well as 'Conservative' in the period before 1922.

Part One: Conservatives and Conservatism

1 The Evolution of the Conservative Party

From Tory to Conservative

Historians have sought the origins of the modern Conservative Party in a variety of periods from the 1660s to the 1860s. Bolingbroke, the Younger Pitt, Burke, Liverpool, Peel and Disraeli have all been claimed as its founding spirit. At the earliest, the lineage of a 'Tory' faction can be traced as far back as the Restoration court of King Charles II, although the 'rage of party' and the division between opposed Tory and Whig groups became most visible after the Glorious Revolution of 1688. Led by Harley and Bolingbroke, the Tories triumphed in the last period of Queen Anne's reign in 1710–14. However, after Anne's death and the arrival of the Hanoverian dynasty they were excluded from power. The connections of some Tories with the exiled Stuart pretenders to the throne and their implication in the Jacobite risings of 1715 and 1745 tarnished the party with treason and drove the name underground. Politics between the 1720s and the 1770s were dominated by the Whigs, whose exclusive hold upon office led to competition amongst themselves and to their sub-division into cliques and factions. After his accession in 1760 King George III was anxious to recover the royal independence which he believed the long ascendancy of Walpole in particular had eroded. In this quest he had only partial success until in December 1783 he turned to William Pitt (known as the Younger Pitt to avoid confusion with his father).

British government from 1783 to 1830 was the almost exclusive preserve of Pitt and his followers. After the French Revolution in 1789 the energies of the ministry were focused upon the threat from a resurgent France and the fear of domestic unrest. The danger posed by revolutionary France also led to powerful denunciations by the Whig intellectual Edmund Burke, from the *Reflections on the Revolution in France* published in 1790 onwards. Burke's articulate and passionate writings gave a moral focus to the instinctive forces of resistance to change. Those concerned to

1

defend property and authority became grouped under Pitt's banner during the 1790s, clarifying the divide in British politics by excluding the Foxites and radicals who called for peace and reform. Pitt never used the term 'Tory' to describe himself, but as supporters of the crown and of social stability and as the staunch opponents of radicals and reformers, Pitt's followers and successors gradually became known as the Tory party. In both attitudes and personnel this body has often been identified as the origin of modern British Conservatism (**2, 10**).

Since 1789 the history of Conservatism has been marked by periods of division and dispute. The first such crisis occurred during the decade which followed the fall of Pitt's ministry in 1801. Some of the Whiggish elements returned to opposition at this point, and later fused with the Foxites. After a short, uneasy peace, war with France resumed and Pitt returned to office in 1804, but his early death in 1806 threw matters back into confusion. The succeeding 'Ministry of all the Talents' foundered upon the issue of religious liberalism in 1807; it was followed by two decades of recognisably Tory administrations under Portland (1807–9), Perceval (1809–12) and Liverpool (1812–27). The latter ministry held together during the period of difficulty and even panic in 1815–22 caused by the strains imposed by the end of the long war, the economic consequences of industrialisation and a run of bad harvests. After the suicide of Castlereagh in 1822, and with fears of revolution from below receding, a strand of 'Liberal Toryism' associated with the rising figure of Canning emerged. Stresses within the ministry were, however, contained until a stroke forced Liverpool's retirement in 1827. Canning succeeded him, but he was a controversial figure whose responsiveness to commercial and urban interests, liberal foreign policy and commitment to redress of Catholic grievances made him unacceptable to hard-line Tories. After his sudden death only four months later, Wellington returned in 1828 to head a divided Tory ministry which depended almost entirely upon Peel to lead in the House of Commons. It was this ministry which faced the problem of Catholic Emancipation in 1829.

Crown and Church were the 'pillars of the constitution' which guaranteed the propertied in the secure enjoyment of their position. The monarchy symbolised hierarchy and order, and loyalty to the symbol of the crown was synonymous with patriotism. The identity of Toryism with the privileges of the established Church of England had become still closer after 1800 under

Sidmouth and Wellington, as the Church came under threat from the spread of Dissent, from the demand for Catholic Emancipation, and from radical secularism and atheism. Resistance to the claims of the Roman Catholics exerted a powerful influence amongst the backbone of Tory support in Parliament and in the country. A dangerous rift opened between them and leading ministers, some of whom were committed to Catholic redress after the undertakings implied by Pitt when the Act of Union was passed in 1800. More acutely, Wellington and Peel had to face the problems of governing Ireland under the pressure of O'Connell's agitation, and their decision to concede emancipation was one of pragmatism rather than principle. Nevertheless, this betrayal outraged the 'Ultra' Protestant Tories in Parliament and much Tory feeling in the country, leaving a deep and lasting scar. Within a few months the passions aroused led to the collapse of the Wellington ministry in 1830.

The leaders of Tory administrations between 1783 and 1830 had not thought of themselves as forming a 'party', for that term denoted faction and irresponsible opposition, and they made no attempt to organise their following. The support of Parliament, where 'independence' was still prized, could never be assumed: this had made the position of the ministry frequently insecure. Pitt, Liverpool, Wellington and Peel saw themselves as 'governing men', owing loyalty to the crown as the King's ministers, and not as mere party figures. However, the loss of the support of William IV in 1830–34 and of Queen Victoria in 1837–41 sent the Tories into the uncharted waters of opposition from which they emerged with a distinct and partisan identity. It could be said that Pitt shaped Toryism itself (despite never using the name), that Peel shaped the Conservatives as a parliamentary party (despite deep personal ambivalence towards the very concept), and that Disraeli added a permanent organisational structure (despite a similarly mixed degree of commitment).

The settlement of the Catholic question and the entry into office of the Whigs under Grey meant that the issue of parliamentary reform now came to the top of the agenda. The struggle over the Reform Bill did not reunite the Tories but further divided them over tactics, policy and leadership. The 'Ultras' remained unreconciled, whilst more moderate Tories were concerned that the lack of representation in Parliament of the populous and prosperous new towns and cities was alienating too much property and influence from the constitution. Even so, Wellington and other Tories were taken aback at the scope of Grey's Bill and determined to resist it. But they lost ground in the 1831 general election, and the House of Lords was forced to pass it by popular pressure and the King's promise to the Whigs to create peers if required. After the general election on the new franchise which followed in 1832 the Tories were left with only 180 MPs to face 480 Reformers, the party's worst result until 1906. The term 'Conservative' had begun to be used by the party's leaders and supporters after 1830, and by 1835 this had replaced 'Tory' as the common party name. 'Tory' has continued to be employed as a more colloquial expression by supporters and opponents alike to this day, although it tends to imply a more instinctive and uncompromising brand of Conservatism.

The age of Peel

In the wake of reform the Conservative Party was divided and defeated, its leaders unpopular and discredited. Yet within a decade the party was restored in vigour, and it recovered a parliamentary majority in the general election of 1841. This rapid reversal of fortune had several causes. There was disillusion amongst middle-class and working-class radicals, for they had expected more from the Reform Act and were demoralised by the weakness and disunity of the Whig ministry after 1834. Nevertheless, the reforms of the 1830s redressed the grievances of the more prosperous and influential sections of the urban middle class, and for many a wish to avoid upheaval displaced their desire for further change. Anglican opinion was alarmed by Whig concessions to radical and Irish pressure over the position of the Church of Ireland, whilst proposals to confiscate the latter's 'surplus' revenue concerned the owners of property everywhere. At the same time the agitation against the new Poor Law, industrial unrest and the rise of Chartism made Conservatism an attractive option. During the 1830s there was a steady 'replacement of reforming enthusiasm by propertied influence' (**9**). But it was the role of Peel and his emergence as the undisputed leader of Conservative opinion which was crucial in building upon these trends. Peel had remained detached during the struggles over reform, but with Wellington in eclipse he was the only possible alternative Prime Minister when William IV dismissed the Whig government in November 1834. Despite royal favour, Peel's ministry could not survive in office in the face of a hostile

Commons majority, but its few months of life marked a crucial stage in the evolution of the Conservative Party. First, it established Peel at the head of the party with unique authority. Second, it brought about the general election of 1835 which marked the start of Conservative electoral recovery. Finally, the need to redefine what the Conservatives stood for and to communicate this clearly to the public led Peel at the start of that election to issue the Tamworth Manifesto. In this he accepted the Reform Act as the final settlement and offered a moderate and constructive Conservatism which both traditional Tories and moderate Whigs could respectably support. It was 'designed to broaden the base of the Conservative Party' (15), and was successful at both the highest and lowest levels. These factors contributed to the steady advance of Conservative support in 1837 and to their victory in 1841.

Immediately on becoming Prime Minister, Peel gave his backbenchers a clear warning that he would follow whichever course he judged to be correct, irrespective of party feeling or interest. In the course of the next four years he proceeded to stretch the loyalty and endurance of his followers beyond the breaking point. After his experience of 1828–32 Peel was inclined to tackle dangerous issues before they became unmanageable: the problem was that this also tended to be before the rest of his party, from their less exalted viewpoint, were convinced of the need to make concessions. As through so much of the history of the Conservative Party, protection and Ireland were the crucial issues. The threat of the ministry's resignation was used to coerce increasingly resentful MPs over several measures, including reductions in tariffs which left the Corn Laws exposed. Peel's attempt to build bridges to the Irish Catholic bishops through extending the public grant to the seminary for priests at Maynooth was especially divisive, and 162 Conservative MPs voted against it. But it was the decision to repeal the protection for agriculture enshrined in the Corn Laws in favour of free trade which finally tore the Conservative Party apart in 1846. The industrial depression of the 1840s and the growth of the urban population had convinced Peel that cheap food was essential and repeal only a matter of time; the 1845 famine in Ireland was not the cause of the decision but provided the spur to action. Once again Peel was riding roughshod over his followers' cherished beliefs, in an apparent gross betrayal of Conservative principles and pledges. Peel's authority ensured that Stanley was the only minister of importance who refused to support him, but the allegiance of the backbenchers had been eroded, and in the crucial division only 112 Conservative MPs supported repeal whilst 231 voted against.

The split in the Conservative Party in 1846 was bitter and permanent. The leading figures around Peel remained detached, and after their mentor's death in 1850 the 'Peelites' coalesced with the Whigs and formed one of the founding elements of the Liberal Party in the 1860s. The year 1846 was 'a watershed' since which 'the history of the Conservative Party proceeds to the present without a break' (**17**). The Protectionist rump at first lacked leadership and organisation, but it was clear that although headless it represented the body and soul of Conservatism, and within a few years there was no dispute over its right to the Conservative name. From 1846 to 1868 the party was led by Stanley, who had gone up to the House of Lords in 1844 and became the 14th Earl of Derby in 1851 (**8**). After some confusion the hitherto disregarded Disraeli emerged as the most powerful debater in the Commons, and by 1852 was the sole leader there. The party which remained after the crisis of 1846 had been driven back into its bastions of the county constituencies and the landed agricultural interest, and its appeal to the urban and industrial sections of society had largely evaporated. Economically and politically this was too narrow a ground, and it locked the Conservatives into the position of permanent opposition for nearly three decades. By the early 1850s it was clear to Disraeli at least that so long as the party remained protectionist it could never appeal to town or industry and could never form a majority government. The Conservatives were only able to take office as a vulnerable minority administration when the Whig, Liberal and radical alliance fell out amongst themselves, as in 1852, 1858–59 and 1866–68. As the one defining feature of those who had repudiated Peel was protection, the emotional and political commitment to this was far from easy to shed and the process was a protracted one. Between 1857 and 1865 Palmerston's combination of a cautious Whig domestic policy and a popular and often pugnacious foreign policy dominated British politics. The Conservative opposition under Derby could find little by way of a distinctive position, and in Parliament their role was often limited to helping the Whig Prime Minister thwart his own radical wing (**17**).

Disraeli and Salisbury

The death of Palmerston in 1865 broke up this mid-Victorian equipoise. It brought more radical figures, Russell and Gladstone, to the leadership of the Liberals. The latter were committed to further parliamentary reform, but the Bill which they proposed in 1866 divided their supporters and led to a further minority Conservative government. Disraeli did not succeed the ageing Derby as Prime Minister until February 1868, but as Commons leader his role was crucial in keeping the ministry afloat. He understood that the Conservatives dared not duck the reform question now that it had been raised, and that by successfully resolving this major issue they could re-establish their credibility as a party of government. Disraeli's settlement of the reform issue increased his and the party's prestige, whilst protecting Conservative electoral interests in the counties. The events of 1867 also launched the powerful if insubstantial myth of 'Tory Democracy'. The parliamentary balance had required Disraeli to accept a greatly extended franchise in the boroughs, but he also had hopes of locating a pool of support lower down the social scale which might be hostile to the traditional Liberalism of most factory owners (**16**). In practice, 'Tory Democracy' amounted to little in the way of a coherent programme, and it was always in tension with the more realistic aim of securing greater support from the middle, professional and business classes in the urban areas. To break ground in this territory, Disraeli encouraged the creation of the main elements of the present-day party organisation: the National Union, founded in 1867, and the Central Office, established in 1870 (**12**). With improved organisation and a greater number of candidates, in 1874 the Conservatives won their first overall majority since Peel's victory of 1841, and it was clear that the Conservative Party was becoming a genuinely national party with an appeal to all communities.

During the twenty years after 1865 the Conservatives completed the long climb back from the status of permanent minority. There were several causes of this, of which the most important was the rise of middle-class 'Villa Toryism' in the towns and the growing suburbs. The ambitious reform programme of Gladstone's ministry in 1868–74 unsettled sections of Whiggish middle-class and professional opinion, especially in London and the Home Counties, whilst success over the Irish Church in 1868 revived the threat of Anglican disestablishment. By the late-nineteenth century the second or third generation of many industrial dynasties had been educated at public school and university, had abandoned Nonconformity for the Church of England, and had purchased country estates on which to follow the lifestyle of the gentleman. As they became socially more integrated into the upper class, so they tended to imbibe its values and adopt the Conservatism which by the 1880s was almost habitual at this level. For these reasons the Conservatives ceased to be the party of the landed and aristocratic interests alone and instead began to take the form of a broader party of business and 'capital'. This process was symbolised by the emergence in Conservative cabinets in the 1870s and 1880s of men from middle-class commercial back-grounds such as W.H. Smith and R.A. Cross. Lower down the scale, the growth of the suburbs encouraged voting on class rather than communal lines by physically separating the social strata (**11**). So too did the rise of a lower-middle class of clerical workers, whose need to express a separate identity from the manual working class often led to both social and political conservatism. However, in an electorate which since 1867 was predominantly working class the Conservatives had to have a wider appeal. In addition to the invocations of 'Tory Democracy', the Conservatives could present themselves as the defenders of working-class independence and pleasures – especially in the matter of drink – against interfering and puritanical Liberalism. Together with the cry of patriotism and pride in empire which appealed to and could unite all classes, this fusion of 'beer and Britannia' was particularly resonant for many middle-aged or older working men in more secure employ-ment: exactly those who qualified to vote under the household franchise. This Conservative advance was assisted by two move-ments which grew alongside the official National Union. The first of these were the Conservative Working-Men's Clubs. Although the Conservatism of many of their members was nominal, they took the name and cause of the party into geographical and social areas it would not otherwise have penetrated. Of more immediate impact was the second body, the Primrose League, founded to foster Disraeli's memory in 1883 and named after his supposedly favourite flower (**65, 68**). It swiftly attracted a large membership, primarily through its social function and a mixture of romantic imagery and deference. The Primrose League and the developing network of constituency associations both reflected and promoted the party spirit which had become widespread in the age of Gladstone and Disraeli. After the Corrupt Practices Act of 1883 imposed strict limits on election expenses, they were crucial in providing a pool of active voluntary workers: the Primrose League's membership included many middle-class women who could raise money and canvass for the party even if they had no vote.

Disraeli's successor, Lord Salisbury, sensed the existence of latent urban Conservatism and this underlay the party's strategy in the Third Reform Act of 1884–85. Use of the blocking power afforded by the growing Conservative preponderance in the House of Lords forced concessions over redistribution. At Salisbury's insistence, almost all districts were divided into single-member seats of roughly equal population size – the first version of the contemporary electoral map. This allowed previously swamped 'islands' of Conservatism to emerge, and in the general election which followed in 1885 the Conservatives won 114 of the 226 English borough seats, a result which would have been inconceivable thirty years before (11). These advances had already occurred before Gladstone's adoption of Irish Home Rule left the Liberals in disarray and led to further substantial Conservative gains in the general election of 1886. An important factor in this was the alliance forged between the Conservatives and those Liberals who refused to follow Gladstone along the path of Home Rule. These Liberal Unionist MPs consisted of two strands: a patrician Whig element led by Hartington, who succeeded as Duke of Devonshire in 1891, and a radical wing led by the controversial Joseph Chamberlain (13). The Liberal Unionists were the medium through which important sections of middle-class Nonconformist Liberalism in the constituencies could respectably adopt a conservative identity. For this reason, despite losses in 1892, Liberal Unionism remained a valuable partner, and in 1895 its leaders entered a coalition cabinet under Salisbury. By the end of the century the Conservative name was being displaced in common usage by the simple term 'Unionist', to denote both the ministry and its supporters in Parliament and in the country. The Irish question, the weakness of the Liberal ministry of 1892–95, and disunity over other issues – in particular, the Boer War – led to Liberal apathy and ineffectiveness, exemplified in the large number of Conservative MPs returned unopposed in the elections of 1895 and 1900. As a result of all these factors, the Conservatives under Salisbury were able to dominate the late-Victorian era, even though his personal brand of Conservatism was defensive and deeply pessimistic, aiming only to stave off for as long as possible the politics of materialism, class hostility and the redistribution of property (14).

Despite its success in the period of 'popular government' and 'democracy' which followed the Third Reform Act, the party's leadership, ethos and support under Salisbury remained no less aristocratic than had been the case in the age of Peel, Derby and Disraeli. During the nineteenth century the Conservatives evolved from the narrow 'Church and King' Toryism of the 1790s to present a wider and more attractive public appeal as the party 'of patriotism, of social order, of political stability, of "Protestantism" and of the security of property' (**10**). However, the defence of the interests identified in the Toryism of Pitt and Liverpool remained central to Conservatism throughout the century. These were the maintenance of the 'ancient constitution' and the privileges which that entailed, the defence of property, the supremacy of the established Church, the prosperity of land and agriculture, and the security of seapower and a predominant share in world trade and colonial interests. In support of these aims, a hierarchical society based upon a popular patriotic spirit was required. Throughout the century, the Conservative road to power frequently lay through alliance with and absorption of disaffected elements of Whiggery and Liberalism, from the Whig schism of 1834 to the rejection of Gladstonian principles by the Liberal Unionists in 1886. Finally, first Disraeli and later Salisbury and Joseph Chamberlain were to add a further and heady element to this brew: a patriotic pride – which opponents labelled 'jingoism' – in Britain's history, in its naval power and in its imperial mission. It was this which led both to Conservative dominance in the last fifteen years of Queen Victoria's reign, and to the Boer War and the problems which followed from this after 1902.

2   Structure and Organisation

The party leader

Any anatomy of the Conservative Party naturally begins at the head, for it is here that executive power is concentrated. The term 'Leader of the Conservative Party' was not officially used until October 1922. Before this there was a leader of the party in the House of Commons and a leader in the House of Lords, separately chosen and formally endorsed by the Conservative members of each House. Whoever became or had been Prime Minister was recognised to be the actual leader of the party, but until such a time or when the party was in opposition a more equal partnership was expected between the two. In practice it was recognised by 1914 that the leader in the House of Commons had to take the tactical initiative and be primarily answerable for the party's policies both in Parliament and upon the public platform. After 1922, Conservative peers participated in the formal meeting at which the new leader of the party was anointed, and since then the leader in the upper House has been appointed and dismissed by the leader of the party.

Until formal rules were devised in 1965, the Conservative leader was selected according to conventions which, although unwritten, were none the less clearly understood. The most important of these was that the choice of a new leader should be a healing and uniting process and not a divisive one (**7**). It was therefore imperative that the issue be settled behind closed doors, and the formal party meetings which took place afterwards were presented with a single agreed candidate – often symbolically nominated through gritted teeth by his defeated rival. Whilst it was therefore technically the case that the parliamentary party chose the leader, the real decision was taken by a handful of front-bench figures – in particular, by the most senior of those not in the running themselves. The field of choice was not large: all Cabinets contain their share of 'elder statesmen' who may be influential but whose day has passed, of capable if uninspiring administrators whom no one considers will rise further, of bores and failures, and of rising juniors who may be spoken of as future contenders but whose day has not yet come. Rarely have there been as many as three or four serious and credible candidates, and often there was only one. This was the case with Balfour in 1902 (for Joseph Chamberlain was both too old and as a Liberal Unionist technically ineligible), with Austen Chamberlain in 1921, and with his half-brother Neville in 1937. Winston Churchill was already Prime Minister and the only possible choice in October 1940, although he had been written off for most of the previous decade (**37**).

During the first five decades of the twentieth century there were only two leadership 'contests'. In 1911 the irreconcilable split between the supporters of Austen Chamberlain and Walter Long led to the decision of both to stand down before the scheduled meeting of MPs (**181, 20**). To avoid this degenerating into chaos and division the two challengers agreed instead to nominate and second the outsider third candidate, Bonar Law, who was then elected unopposed. In 1923, whoever King George V invited to become Prime Minister after the final collapse of Bonar Law's health would also therefore replace the latter as party leader. The choice lay between Stanley Baldwin, leading figure in the Commons, and Lord Curzon, the leader in the Lords. After taking advice from some senior Conservatives the monarch opted for Baldwin, in part because he was personally more acceptable to his Cabinet colleagues. There has been much controversy over who influenced the King, but it is clear that the rise of the Labour Party to become the principal opposition, and their lack of a presence in the Lords, made him regard the choice of Curzon as too provocative (**45, 143, 176**). A lengthy apprenticeship as heir apparent does not seem to have been an asset: Balfour, and Austen and Neville Chamberlain all turned out to be disasters who did not win a single election between them. Rather, it was the three 'unexpected' leaders – Bonar Law, Baldwin and Churchill – who enjoyed lengthy reigns and electoral success.

In theory the leader had absolute discretion over policy, which only he had the right to define, but in fact there were several practical limitations upon this. Resignations or rebellions could damage the leader's authority and imperil the party's electoral chances. The leader had to try to maintain a consensus amongst the senior figures in the parliamentary party and was expected to include those who carried weight in the House or with the public in his real or shadow cabinet. He also needed to carry the support of the backbenchers and of the rank and file outside Westminster.

The scope of government activity became too complex after 1900 for the full range of affairs to be mastered by one person; more responsibility had to be devolved to front-bench colleagues who had relevant experience. By the 1930s, and still more after 1945, policy-making had become a more collegiate matter, in which many individuals and institutions within the party played a part (**7**).

Leaders of the Conservative Party have always been vulnerable after electoral defeat, especially when they have been out of harmony with the more partisan desires of their followers. There was also no formal machinery for challenging or deposing leaders, but this made their removal difficult rather than impossible. It certainly helped a leader to ride out the storms, as Balfour did in 1906–11 and Baldwin in 1923–24 and 1929–30. Both leaders remained in place because there was a lack of a suitable successor, because each in their own way had a unique national prestige, and because many in the party remained loyal, due to dislike of the motives and methods of those who clamoured against them. Four things could render a leader's position so untenable that resignation would be the only possible course. The first of these was a rejection by the Cabinet or shadow cabinet of their leadership or of a key position to which they were personally committed: if all or even most of the major figures were involved, the leader could hardly carry on. This could also be a way of forcing a change in policy rather than of leader: in January 1913 Bonar Law was persuaded to remain despite the rejection of his tariff policy, whilst ten years later he was talked out of resigning as Prime Minister when the Cabinet did not support his desire to reject the American war-debt settlement (**20**). In 1939, the threat of a Cabinet mutiny forced Neville Chamberlain's hand over the declaration of war after the German attack on Poland. Second, on several occasions during this period leaders summoned a 'party meeting', either just of MPs or also including peers and prospective parliamentary candidates. Some of these meetings were unavoidable, such as in February 1906 (to settle policy and leadership after a catastrophic electoral defeat) or in August 1931 (to endorse the decision to join the National Government). In other cases the leaders called such gatherings when it tactically suited them to confront and defeat their critics (**132**). However, the strategy was a risky one: the loss of the vote on any such occasion would instantly terminate a leadership, as occurred in October 1922.

Third, a rebellion in the parliamentary party which spread beyond a particular disaffected section to include the broad centre would almost certainly undermine a leader, and perhaps cause a front-bench revolt. It was for this reason that the dissidence of the 'diehard' right was not a serious danger in 1920–21 or over India in 1933–35, but was potentially fatal when their revolt threatened to spread to the ranks of normally loyal and steady MPs in 1922 and 1930. The attack of the anti-appeasers upon Neville Chamberlain followed the same pattern, making little headway until the failure of his foreign policy in 1939 and the military débâcles of 1940 convinced others to vote with them or to abstain (**152**). The fourth possible cause of a leader's fall was more problematic, but a vote of no confidence from the National Union either at national level or even from a key region, whilst having no formal authority, would have been such a serious rebuff as to make the leader's position almost untenable. This nearly happened on several occasions: in 1905 the annual conference was restrained only with difficulty from repudiating Balfour's fragile compromise position on tariff reform, whilst the likely fractiousness of the forthcoming 1911 conference was a factor in Balfour's final decision to quit. In 1922 Austen Chamberlain called the party meeting at the Carlton Club in order to pre-empt that year's annual conference, and both Bonar Law in December 1912 and Baldwin in October 1930 were nearly forced from the leadership by open disavowal of their tariff policy by the powerful north-west region of the National Union. It is also clear that the party managers were worried about the danger of losing the vote on the India question at the annual conference or at the Central Council in 1933–35. This did not happen, but any leader would have found it very difficult to carry on with a wide and growing rift opening between the front-bench elite and their followers. If a leader tried to do so, as Austen Chamberlain found in 1922, it was likely that he would be seen as a threat to the unity and survival of the party. Not only would MPs rebel, but even normally loyal institutions such as the whips and the Central Office would turn against him [**doc. 14**]. Problems of health have forced the resignations of Conservative leaders more often than defeat or revolt, and a combination of physical stamina and mental willpower was crucial. Since 1868 only Baldwin has departed at the moment of his own choice, apparently successful and still in reasonable health.

The parliamentary party

The Conservative membership of the House of Commons between

1902 and 1951 consisted of four different elements. First were the front-bench leaders, serving or former Cabinet ministers. Below this was the party's 'middle management' of junior ministers and whips, and the Parliamentary Private Secretaries whose feet were on the bottom rung of the ladder of promotion. The third group were the long-serving backbench MPs, the 'knights of the shires' who had represented the safer seats for as long as two or three decades. Most of these were not career politicians, but although not outstanding in intellect or debating skill many were respected by their colleagues for the virtues of dependability and straight-forwardness. They combined seniority of service and comparative detachment with the possession of opinions which mirrored those of the party's natural supporters. As a result, they were often regarded as being the embodiment of its soul. When Sir Samuel Hoare organised a select meeting of just such MPs on the day before the Carlton Club meeting of 1922, it was the names and not the number which impressed Bonar Law and encouraged him to come forward and head the revolt against the Coalition (**51**). The fourth and final element were not greatly different, but their presence was more ephemeral: these were the MPs for marginal seats whom victory or defeat washed in and out of Parliament. After the Conservative landslides of 1918, 1924 and 1931 there were many who sat for a single term and never reappeared. Given the nature of their seats, this group tended naturally to press for centrist policies and pacts or alliances.

The organisation of parliamentary business when the party was in office, and the maintenance of attendance and discipline, were the duty of the Chief Whip. He was assisted by five or six junior whips and from the 1920s by a further two or three assistant whips. These posts were part of the upwards ladder and paralleled the junior ministerial posts, but the whips' room could often be a career in itself. Social status was an important qualification: whips tended to come from the landed aristocracy and gentry and the officer class (**179, 181**). The role of the whips was more one of persuasion than coercion, and their disciplinary powers should not be exaggerated. Most MPs at most times wanted to stay loyal, to keep the party united and to follow the advice of their leaders and the guidance of the whips. The latter had few sanctions they could apply to rebels who were not ambitious for office. It was the constituency associations which had the power to select and to deselect candidates, and provided that local support was retained – and dissent in a 'rightwards' direction was customarily given a good deal of tolerance – the whips could do little. Punitive withdrawals of the whip were very rare and more symbolic than effective (**54**).

The only backbench faction to have a long-term existence in this period was the 'diehards'. This began with those resolutely opposed to acceptance of the Parliament Act of 1911, but after 1918 the label identified a cohesive and informally organised group of right-wing MPs. They numbered around 40 through most of the 1920s, rising as high as 70 on the one issue of India in the 1931–35 parliament. The relative strength of the 'diehard' wing increased when the party was defeated, as they were better represented in the safe seats. They therefore suffered proportionately fewer losses, and so for example in 1929 the right wing rose from one-seventh to one-fifth (**6**). This tendency was unhelpful, for it inclined the party away from the tone needed to recapture lost ground at the next election and so return to office. However, in other respects it was less of a problem for the leadership than might be supposed, as the large majority of backbench MPs were normally moderate and loyal supporters. The prospect of imminent electoral disaster could make the backbenchers restive or apathetic, but they rarely considered the alternative leaders available to be better than the existing ones, and they tended to complain rather than to revolt (**169**). Rebellions when they did occur revolved around specific issues and waxed and waned accordingly.

Channels of communication between front and back benches also improved during this period. The First World War was an important stimulus with the formation of the backbench 'ginger groups' of the Unionist Business Committee in 1915 and the larger Unionist War Committee in 1916 (**52**). After 1918 these unofficial bodies faded away, but when in opposition in early 1924 the leadership introduced an official structure which was to take permanent form. These were the backbench 'subject' committees, each of which covered the brief of a major government department (**4, 7**). Led at first by the relevant ex-minister, they assisted in the formulation of a new party programme. When these ministers returned to office after the Conservative victory in the 1924 election, the subject committees continued under the chairmanship of prominent backbenchers. They were open to all MPs, and at times of crisis numbers swelled to become important sounding boards of parliamentary opinion which the whips closely monitored. Finally, one unofficial initiative slowly came to have an official status: the 1922 Committee. The origins of this body have been frequently misunderstood. It was actually founded in April 1923 by a group of MPs who had entered the House for the first time in the general election of November 1922: the date in the title refers to the intake and not, as is often wrongly assumed, to the fall of the Lloyd George Coalition. The Committee was intended to help the new boys to find their feet, but unlike similar bodies it did not then wither away. The 1923 and 1924 elections produced further new intakes, and membership was extended to all Conservative backbenchers in 1926. The whips found it to be useful in several ways, and the 1922 Committee provided a forum for the expression of the loyalty of the moderate mainstream. However, between 1926 and 1939 it was not politically important, being at times little more than a lecture club, and it only began to take on its modern role and prominence during the wartime coalition and in the post-war period of 1945–51 (**50**).

Conservative MPs were drawn from the upper classes. They tended either to be connected to landed and titled families or to be successful local figures who came into the House after making a name in business or in the professions (**7, 53**). Over the period as a whole, the proportion of those from the more traditional backgrounds declined and those from business and industry rose. These adjustments of emphasis within the elite reflected economic change but hardly indicated a social revolution (**6, 56**):

Occupations of Conservative MPs	*1914 (%)*	*1939 (%)*
Landowners	23	10
Armed, Colonial and Diplomatic Services	22	19
Professional	36	32
Finance and commerce	14	23
Manufacturing industry	10	18

Local associations expected their candidates to be men of standing and of means. They normally had to provide the expenses for each election, to pay a substantial annual subscription to the constituency association, to be open-handed in support of local events and charities, and of course to maintain themselves. The introduction of a relatively small salary for MPs in 1912 made little difference to this state of affairs. Safe seats could afford to pick and choose, and the inter-war period saw many complaints of nominations being auctioned to the highest bidder, regardless of other qualifications. After the extension of the franchise in 1918 there were frequent exhortations for the selection of more able but poorer candidates. Although these had little immediate effect, they created a climate of opinion which led to change. In 1935 the list of approved candidates was established, from which constituencies had to select if their choice was to receive official recognition and support. The most significant reform of all occurred after the Maxwell-Fyfe Committee Report of 1949, which required the association to fund the election expenses and forbade all but a token subscription from the candidate (7). This altered the balance between money and talent but did not much change the preferences or prejudices of selection committees, who tended to consider that their locality was not in some way an appropriate one for a working man. Women candidates were slightly less rare, but they were mainly confined to the difficult or hopeless contests. Only three women sat for reasonably safe seats between the wars; all were titled ladies adopted by constituencies which their husband had represented before going up to the House of Lords. However, the unrepresentative social character of the parliamentary party does not seem to have deterred voters or prevented electoral success. In the more deferential society of pre-war Britain, many electors expected a candidate to possess status, experience, and the confident public manner these provided.

Central Office and the party organisation

The Conservative Party organisation outside Parliament is divided into two separate elements which exist in parallel and normally in harmony. The first of these is the professional salaried staff in the Central Office, the 'party machine'; the second is the representative institutions of the voluntary membership in the National Union, the 'rank and file'. The basic structure of the modern Conservative Party evolved in the course of the nineteenth century; since then it has adapted to changes in the electoral system and to defeats.

Conservative Central Office was established in 1870, and from then until 1911 a small staff headed by the Principal Agent worked under the overall supervision of the Chief Whip, whose responsibilities embraced all aspects of party management. By 1902 this burden had become too great for any individual, and the Victorian system proved unable to cope with the stresses of the following decade. Rank-and-file enthusiasm for tariff reform between 1903 and 1906 led to tensions between the National Union and the Central Office, which was directly responsible to Balfour. The latter was forced to make limited concessions to popular control after the disastrous election of 1906, but the two further defeats of 1910 made fundamental changes unavoidable (**62**). Balfour appointed the Unionist Organisation Committee, and its report in April 1911 established the framework which still exists. The responsibilities of the Chief Whip were limited to the House of Commons, and two new posts were created: a 'Chairman of the Party Organisation' to manage Central Office, and a Treasurer to take charge of the funds. The Chairman of the Party was supposed to be a figure of Cabinet rank, but in fact only two of the Chairmen between 1911 and 1951 had such status: Neville Chamberlain, who served a short term under special circum-stances in 1930–31, and Lord Woolton in 1946–55. The others were drawn from the ranks of the junior ministers, and their role varied between backroom administrator and personal aide to the party leader, who alone appointed them. The Party Chairman only had direct control over the officials of Central Office and its regional outposts. Although between 1911 and 1930 the Party Chairman also chaired the meetings of the Executive Committee of the National Union, he had no power to give orders to the local associations and could only employ persuasion and encourage-ment (**7**).

The principal function of Central Office was to provide assis-tance to the localities, and in particular to the marginal and weaker seats. Its original task had been to place suitable candidates in all constituencies, where necessary by providing financial support. It also arranged the printing of the millions of leaflets and posters which were used between and during election campaigns (**6**). In the inter-war period, Central Office coordinated an increas-ingly elaborate range of activities which included a staff of profes-sional speakers, the training and placing of agents, specialist sections for women and trade unionists, various party journals and other services to the divisional associations. In the 1930s there was even a fleet of mobile cinema vans showing specially-made films; these proved particularly popular in rural seats (**61**). Central Office was revitalised and expanded by the first Chairman, Steel-Maitland, between 1911 and 1914. After the 1918 Reform Act, new departments were added and the lines of responsibility became confused, and when Davidson became Chairman in 1926 he initiated a fundamental review. The result of its report was the establishment in 1927 of a structure which remained in place until the 1970s (**7**). Two main directorates were established, one dealing with all organisational matters and the other with publications and propaganda. The most senior official at the Central Office was the Principal Agent, and in the further reorganisation of 1931 this post was given authority over all departments and retitled as 'General Director'.

After the defeat of 1929, two important additions were made to the central party organisation. The first of these reflected concern over the nature of the democratic electorate created in 1918 and the need for political education to raise the mettle of the rank and file and equip them for the fray. In 1930 Davidson raised sufficient funds to purchase the Ashridge estate, which, as the Bonar Law Memorial College, provided short residential courses for activists sent by their local association; it was requisitioned in the war, but a similar centre was opened at Swinton in 1948. The second initiative was the more important and to prove of lasting significance: the founding of the Conservative Research Department in 1930 (**59**). As a consequence of the greater role and higher public expectations of government, detailed policy-making had become more essential in the 1920s. In its first incarnation under the close control of Neville Chamberlain between 1930 and 1939, and again when restored under R.A. Butler after the 1945 election, the CRD provided the raw materials of Conservative policy (**66**). In December 1945 Butler established the Conservative Political Centre, which was intended to foster political education at all levels of the party (**4, 161**). With all these initiatives the Central Office staff expanded from half a dozen in 1902 to 180 in 1928 and, after a reduction in the 1930s, to nearly 250 by 1951. These figures did not include the important network of regional offices through which close liaison with the individual constituencies was maintained and grass-roots opinion monitored. England and Wales were divided into twelve Areas, each of which had a Central Office Area Agent with supporting staff and premises (**7**). The organisation of the party in Scotland was quite separate, and from 1911 it was directed by the parliamentary Scottish Whip through his Political Secretary and a staff based in Edinburgh (**69**). The regional tier had no direct authority over the local associations, but an effective Area Agent could acquire considerable influence by providing practical help and as the channel through whom central funds were disbursed.

The National Union and the rank and file

The National Union was the representative body of the voluntary membership outside Parliament. It had been founded in 1867 to organise support in the boroughs, and by 1902 there was a recognised and affiliated local association in every constituency in the country (**64**). The National Union had no formal role in the selection of the leader or in the framing of policy, but through its various organs, and more immediately through their MP, the local rank and file could exert a powerful influence upon the direction taken by the party. Resolutions were debated at its annual conference, which had an attendance of several thousand; although their text was rarely controversial, the 'tone' of the discussion could carry a clear message. Franker views could also be aired in the less public forums of the National Union's Central Council and its Executive Committee. Between 1911 and 1951 both of these steadily grew in size, and as they became more cumbersome they met less frequently. In 1902 the Council was a compact body of around 30, which met nine times a year, but after 1919 it became a mini-conference with an average attendance of around 700, between the wars meeting twice a year and after 1945 only once. Similarly, the Executive grew from a gathering of six to twelve before 1906 to a possible 156 by 1951, whilst the number of sessions halved (**7**).

Below this, the various 'specialist' wings of the party each had their own regional and national Advisory Committees, a process which began with those for women and for trade unionists in 1919. The party's youth movement, the Junior Imperial League, had a separate existence from its foundation in 1906 until the Second World War, after which it was reformed as the Young Conservatives and fully integrated into the National Union at all levels (**63**). The regional organisation of the National Union had been established in the 1880s, when England and Wales were divided into ten Provincial Divisions, but after 1906 this structure dissolved into ineffective confusion with separate Divisions for almost every county. Between 1925 and 1937 these were slowly regrouped into Provincial Areas, which under rules adopted in 1930 matched the territory of the Central Office Areas. The regional organisation gradually became more important and active between the wars, but some Areas had a greater feeling of solidarity and cooperation than others.

The key unit of organisation in the Conservative Party was the constituency association. These jealousy guarded their autonomy both within their own locality and in their relations with the central hierarchy, especially over finance and candidate selection. Successful reforms, such as the Maxwell-Fyfe Reports of 1948–49, recognised this [**doc. 26**] and worked through consensus and persuasion: inefficient or rebellious associations could not be disbanded, except in rare cases where they broke up or infringed the rules of procedure (**7**). The most important figure at local level was the association chairman, who supervised its affairs on a daily basis and chaired the meetings of its central body (normally the Executive Committee but in some places the Council). After 1918 this was often supplemented by a Women's Committee, Finance Committee and other sub-committees; there was normally also a structure of district branches for each ward or polling district (**7**). In the Edwardian period constituency activity was primarily concerned with electoral registration: with a limited and complex franchise it was crucial to support the claims of Conservatives to the vote and to contest those of likely opponents. After the 1918 Act this ceased to be important, and associations developed a range of propaganda and social functions intended to rally Conservative supporters and to raise money. These in turn attracted a large membership, although between the wars the number of subscribers was often limited to a narrow local elite (**6**). After 1945 massive recruitment drives were launched, not only to restore membership levels but also to encourage the more active participation of an army of small subscribers. Throughout the period most constituencies were able to employ a full-time professional agent, who in turn ensured the continuing effectiveness of the local organisation. In the late 1930s there were 390 serving agents, and in the post-war revival a peak of more than 500 was reached in the early 1950s. Although there were areas where Conservatism was weak and the organisation was on a skeleton basis, the party had an effective presence in all regions and types of constituency.

The strength of the Conservative Party organisation derived directly from the nature and extent of its social support, which provided the two essential components of money and a reservoir of committed voluntary workers. At local level the Conservatives recruited their leadership from the upper and upper-middle classes, of whom after 1918 only a minority remained Liberal and a mere handful supported Labour. These groups provided the Conservative Party with social prestige, traditions of local leadership and public service, and the deferential response that these elicited from many of those in less exalted stations in life. They also furnished the munitions of political warfare: influence, financial backing, the support of the local press and a large supply of prospective candidates who were educated, socially respectable and could pay their own way. However, in the age of the mass electorate the support of much of the lower-middle class was equally crucial to the Conservative cause. This section provided most of the active membership of the constituency associations, especially at branch level and amongst the women and the Junior Imperial League, the precursor of the post-war Young Conservatives; this gave the party a living presence at the grass roots which money alone could never have created. Working-class members proved much harder to recruit or retain, and, whilst they clearly existed, their role was mainly a passive one. The Conservative trade-unionist movement established after 1918 never amounted to much, despite receiving lavish encouragement and support from the party hierarchy and Central Office. Many constituencies resisted forming a local 'Labour Advisory Committee'; they disliked the concept of a class-based movement, and contact with its personnel was often socially uncomfortable (**6, 7**). Where such committees did exist their membership was usually small and dependent upon financial help with the costs of meetings and travel; many became self-enclosed cliques or were disregarded and withered away. The Conservative Clubs had many more members, but by the 1920s they had almost ceased to have any worthwhile political role. Attempts to revive this or create parallel movements such as the National Conservative League, active in some regions in the 1920s, all met with failure.

Women first became involved in voluntary work for the party through the Primrose League between 1883 and 1914 (**65**), although even before the First World War this was being displaced by constituency association branches for women. The massive recruitment of women after the granting of the vote in 1918 built on this foundation, but was also due to the facilities which the party provided for social integration in a respectable cause. Conservative women's branches, especially in suburban and rural districts, were not run by working women from shop or factory but by married women, often middle-aged or older, and generally middle-class with a leavening of upper-class ladies at the top (**5**). These women had the leisure to engage in a round of social and charitable activities, in which the Conservative Party complemented the Mothers' Union, the Women's Institute and so on.

Women provided the party with assiduous fund-raisers, with voluntary workers for committee rooms and canvassing, with the organisers of fêtes, bazaars, whist drives and other social functions, but not with leadership. Political discussion was still the prerogative of the numerically much smaller men's branches. By the late 1920s local joint Executive Committees had become the norm in most constituencies, but the chairman and leading figures would still almost invariably be men, as would the candidate. However, this was socially respectable and seems to have caused little friction. By the end of the 1920s it was claimed that the women's side of the Conservative Party had more than a million members (**7**).

3 Conservatism

The nature of Conservatism

After the Corrupt Practices legislation of 1883 and the extensions
of the franchise in 1884 and 1918, political parties had to depend
upon the voluntary participation of a mass membership. To
succeed, a party required an appeal which would attract the
sympathy of a cross-section of society and inspire a proportion of
those people to active involvement. Only for a few could there be
direct rewards, such as a parliamentary career or the receipt of
honours and preferment. The majority who gave their time or
money were motivated by a mixture of positive and negative forces.
The latter derived from the suspicion and fear which the apparent
alternatives provoked, the former from the meshing of
Conservative thought and attitudes with culture and society as a
whole (**145**). Conservative ideas have too often been treated as if
the very concept was a contradiction in terms, but any discussion
limited to leaders, organisation and events overlooks a vital part of
the equation. In order to understand three key aspects of the
twentieth-century Conservative Party – the nature of its policies, its
electoral appeal under a democratic franchise, its cohesion and
resilience – the principles and prejudices which underlie them
must also be illuminated.

Although the Conservatives did not place the same emphasis on
ideology as their rivals, a considerable literature about the nature
and aspirations of Conservatism was produced between 1902 and
1951. Much of this was intended for a general audience through
short books, pamphlets and articles in the periodical press, in
many cases penned by active politicians. The two most influential
works were Lord Hugh Cecil's *Conservatism* (1912) and Quintin
Hogg's *The Case for Conservatism* (1947); between these the flavour
of inter-war Conservatism was best conveyed by the published
volumes of Stanley Baldwin's speeches (**74, 79**). Conservatism
consists of broad attitudes rather than specific principles. It is a
matter of temperament rather than ideology, and for that reason

has always been hard to pin down. There has been no tradition of internal debate: most of the works on Conservatism were written as personal statements, and apart from conventional genuflections to Burke or Disraeli they did not engage with one another. Nor did Conservatives tend to formulate detailed policies and programmes; blueprints for action were naturally inappropriate to the party which wished to preserve the *status quo* (7).

This lack of precision can be misinterpreted as mere pragmatism, as if the party's only principle was to gain and keep power. Of course, that is important to any party and particularly to one opposed to change – to bar the way to opponents would on its own be a reasonable purpose. In fact, Conservative politics were much more complex than that simple model suggests, as demonstrated by the stresses within the party, the periodic tension between the grass roots and their leaders, and the spells in opposition. The loyalty and deference which the party's rank and file normally accorded its leaders allowed them some room for manoeuvre. There has always been a tendency to accept that Conservatism is what Conservative leaders and governments deliver, and they were usually given a substantial benefit of the doubt – but not an unlimited one. Leaders who did not respect the party's instincts, interests or traditions found the ground giving way beneath their feet, as in 1846, 1911, 1922, 1940 and 1975. Pragmatism alone was not enough to inspire a following. When moderation and caution became too predominant in the party's image, as in 1928–30, the result was apathy in the constituencies, electoral defeat, and consequently a serious backlash which threatened to unseat the leader. In fact, Conservatives have never felt comfortable with any really pragmatic government. Even in wartime the party was often restive with decisions based upon expediency, such as over Irish conscription in 1917–18 or the fate of Poland and eastern Europe in 1944–45. The most pragmatic peacetime ministry of modern times, the Lloyd George Coalition of 1918–22, alienated most Conservative MPs and was brought down by antagonistic party feeling from below, whilst Balfour's cautious middle way on protection between 1903 and 1906 hardly fared any better.

Between the two extremes of rootless expediency and rigid ideology, the Conservative Party had 'a distinctive character and organisational purpose'. In the service of the economic and social groups whose interests the party existed to defend and maintain, it was founded upon the combination of 'an intellectual approach and an emotional appeal' (**77**). British Conservatism has never been based upon any systematic doctrine – a situation which both its adherents and its critics regard as a source of strength. This does not mean that it lacked consistency or coherence, and several mutually supporting themes can be identified as characteristic of the Conservative frame of mind in the first half of the twentieth century. The first of these was 'natural conservatism', which Hugh Cecil defined as distrust of the unknown and love of the familiar [**doc. 1**]. Fear of change could be both a product of personal temperament and of social and economic status; of outlook, age and experience as much as of the possession of property or of the peril of descent into a lower class. It was therefore widely diffused throughout the whole population, and this feeling may well have been strongest in the case of the less confident, the less educated, and those in modest but respectable circumstances. Small property as well as large felt threatened by social upheaval and a collapse of law and order or of accepted morality and status. The families of tradesmen, clerks, managers, shopkeepers and small businessmen often felt the least secure, for they lacked the physical distance and financial reserves which in some respects insulated the upper class. Their own personal experience, and the recognition that humanity existed in a disorderly world, led many people of all types to the conscious or unconscious conclusion that 'the facts of life are Tory'.

One of the most important Conservative themes was that of respect for the traditions of the past and therefore of structures which had been shaped by use. The pillars of society were not the property of the present to dispose of as they pleased, but were to be held in trust for future generations. Institutions which had met the test of time should not be lightly cast away for some passing fad or theory. Before the First World War the Church of England was regarded as one of the two principal guarantors of continuity: it symbolised not only property, authority and stability but also national identity against foreign domination. It was 'ancient, aristocratic and peculiarly English'; by joining Church and state its position as the established Church was an assurance to many Conservatives of strong Christian feeling that a religious basis to national life would be preserved (**77, 7**). The second guarantor was the historic constitution. It lay at the centre of the Conservatives' view of society and shielded everything else which they sought to conserve. The rule of law depended upon and at the same time supported the constitution and the maintenance of order and security. The English common law had evolved by custom and precedent over many centuries and thus was peculiarly suited to the national needs. It acted as a vital bulwark of individual freedom and property by preventing abuse from the powerful, by holding institutions to their responsibilities, by providing channels for grievance and redress, and by securing a cohesive community (**4**). Property was defended because it also ensured stability, whilst any attack upon it would lead to loss of confidence, economic depression and ultimately social disintegration, as different groups wrangled over the spoils.

Conservative instincts

The three principles enunciated by Disraeli in 1872 remained the most commonly accepted definition of Conservative aims during the first half of the twentieth century. To the traditional defence of the established order and constitution Disraeli had added two further points: the preservation of the empire and the improvement of the condition of the people. Both of these in their different ways evoked the theme of patriotism, and after the internal and external problems revealed in the 1890s they became even more closely linked in the concept of 'social imperialism', fuelled by Darwinian fears for national survival. The imperial cry was an uncomplicated matter for most Conservatives, being simply the extension of patriotic nationalism to a wider field. This had become a distinctive element in the Conservatives' appeal since 1865, and a matter of pointed contrast with their opponents. The Conservative Party's self-identification with patriotism was intense: it could neither recognise nor accept different flavours. Liberals and Socialists were 'little Englanders' whose irresolute weakness would leave British interests overseas vulnerable to hardier competitors and permit national defences to fall into disrepair. They were accused of always taking the foreigner's side against their own, and sometimes – as with radical 'pro-Boers' in 1900 – almost of treason. The Conservative Party gained great dividends both electorally and in terms of unity and a sense of purpose from 'wrapping itself in the flag' – quite literally, as the Union Jack was draped over the platform at meetings and used without blush or restraint in the party's publications. Patriotism and pride in the empire 'upon which the sun never sets' were forces which could defuse class antagonism: 'what unites all classes is loyalty to the nation and what touches men of all ranks is symbolic representation of the nation: the monarch, the flag, the anthem' (**79**). By 1902 the term 'Unionist' had largely supplanted 'Conservative' in the party's own vocabulary, and the latter did not become common currency again until the mid-1920s. Unionism was meant by many of its English, Scottish and Welsh adherents to embrace much wider concerns than just the defence of the Act of Union with Ireland: it was a doctrine which aimed to secure unity between classes, unity between the different parts of the British Isles, and unity within the empire.

The 'condition of the people' raised more complex problems. At one level it amounted to no more than a rehearsal of the Tory tradition of practical and undogmatic reform: factory and sanitation Acts, recognition of limited trade-union rights, housing and local government reform, and so on. This could be cited as proof that Conservatism was far from inimical to the working class and even contrasted with the moralistic, rigid, interfering Liberal style. If this seemed to be the small change of administrative reform, there was the sweeping and romantic appeal of the 'Tory Democracy' of Disraeli and Lord Randolph Churchill. This was largely a myth, but still one which retained a powerful tug upon Conservative sentiment, and which later figures could invoke in their support. However, whilst the rhetoric of the Conservative Party has often been Disraelian, its practice in power has far more often echoed the pragmatism of Peel. Social reform became more problematic after 1902, as it brought the party face to face with collectivist ideas and with the problem of the role of the state. Conservatives favoured liberty, but did not believe that it was an economic matter or that it was directly linked to equality. The latter they viewed as both unworkable and undesirable, instead accepting a hierarchical society as the natural state. Authority and initiative should flow from those above who were most capable of providing it. In the Disraelian era this 'natural aristocracy' was equatable with the landed peerage, but by the inter-war period it also embraced the 'captains of industry', those with the talent to create wealth and prosperity not just for themselves but for many dependent upon them.

Conservatives believed that society was a living organism which was too complex to be understood from a merely human perspective (**7**). It was not a mechanical structure to be tinkered with or redesigned, for that was more likely to be destructive than constructive. This analysis was closely linked to the religious basis of Conservatism: mankind could not and should not assume the functions of the Creator. The Conservatives' emphasis upon man as a fallen being came from the same context and was fundamental to their attitudes to social policy and collective state action. The imperfection of human nature meant that the tendency to evil rather than good could not be ignored. Grand schemes of social engineering failed to allow for human envy, greed, fear, ignorance and superstition. They were foredoomed to failure, but Conservatives feared the cost of experiments which would shatter or weaken the bulwarks against chaos erected by the wisdom of centuries. The Conservative frame of mind was one of pessimism, and the contrast with liberal optimism was apparent in responses not only to domestic matters but also to foreign affairs. Conservatives preferred the 'realism' of the balance of power to the 'idealism' of the Gladstonian 'Concert of Europe' or its inter-war successor the League of Nations. They were deeply sceptical of the power of reason, and distrusted the inflexibility of the social theories and programmes which emanated from that perspective. To Conservatives they combined vaulting ambition with rigid impracticality, and from Rousseau to Lenin their hallmark appeared to be an arrogant dismissal of the past combined with contempt for the individual. In the Conservative mentality the emphasis was placed not upon the generic 'rights of man' but upon the duties of the individual.

There were no universal panaceas: Conservatives had no belief in the power of politics to remedy the problems of the world [**doc. 2**]. It followed from this that the state 'should operate to provide the proper environment, with the appropriate amount of freedom, for the progressive development of human character' (**80**). Conservatives were not hostile to the existence of state authority when codified by law and custom, for without these security and stability would not exist. They were concerned instead about the potential development of an over-mighty state and the misuses to which executive power could be put. The preservation of substantial private property which would form a ballast in society was the best defence against this, and thus social inequality was deemed an acceptable price to pay to avoid tyranny. In the Conservative view any active role of the state in domestic social or economic matters would require intrusive powers: hence the reference to 'some form of Gestapo' in Churchill's election broadcast of 1945. The implementation of such measures would in turn necessitate a massive, unaccountable bureaucracy which would be ruinously costly in taxation. The urban businessmen and suburban ratepayers who migrated to the Conservative Party from the mid-nineteenth century brought with them the Liberal ethic of cheap and minimal government. By the first decade of the twentieth century hostility to collectivism was emerging as a strong theme in Conservative thought (**7, 76**). The demand for 'economy' in local and national expenditure became a potent one amongst the rank and file, especially after the growth of government and the increased tax burden which were caused by the First World War. Freedom of capital and market were important but, as Eden told the 1947 conference, 'we are not a party of unbridled, brutal capitalism, and never have been'.

The Conservatives remained more authoritarian in their attitudes to the state than the Liberals, and more pragmatic. They accepted extensions of the role of government not through conviction but through necessity. Under the pressure of prolonged total war, Conservatives tended to suspend all normal rules and subordinate other issues to the overriding patriotic impulse that the war must be prosecuted with the utmost rigour and fullest commitment of resources. Authority was taken to provide manpower through conscription and to control industrial production, transport, the rationing of food and other goods, the movement of citizens, the internment of aliens and the censorship of the press. Conservatives were willing to adopt compulsion, but at the same time were careful to ensure compensation for infringements of property rights. Where government assumed the direction of private industry a 'normal' rate of return for owners and shareholders had to be furnished, but anything in the nature of wartime 'profiteering' offended against patriotism and aroused Conservative hostility. In both 1914–18 and 1939–45 there was a reaction after the war and a desire to return to 'normality', and thus rapidly to dismantle the structures which had been built up during the hostilities.

The power of the state was used even more empirically in peacetime. The readoption of protectionism in the Edwardian era was both a response to the weaknesses in Britain's world position and an ideological alternative to the mixture of free-trade individualism and state intervention which made up the 'New Liberalism'. Tariff reform was itself a form of collectivist economic interference which sought to influence supply and demand and to channel them in directions desired for wider national or imperial reasons. Protective duties to defend industry were justified by the cry of unfair (which usually simply meant succcessful) foreign competition, and the claim that imposing them would promote rationalisation of old or inefficient plant. Conservative ministers between the wars employed a variety of measures to tackle Britain's economic stagnation, including import quotas, subsidies, regional aid, rationalisation schemes and marketing boards. However, it was not until the final stages of the Second World War that some leading figures, influenced by the spreading Keynesian orthodoxy, came to believe that government either could or should manage the economy. A similar Peelite acceptance of changes which had become part of the political landscape shaped the response to the welfare measures introduced before 1914. When the Conservatives returned to power in the 1920s they did not seek to repeal them, and in the 1924–29 government they embarked upon widows' pensions, factory and poor-law reform, and other issues. The intentions of these and similar measures should not be misunderstood. They represented two elements in Conservatism: the emotional desire for 'fair play' and the practical tactic of maintaining the efficiency and popular legitimacy of government. They did not add up either to corporatism or to a desire for a 'mixed' economy or 'managed capitalism'. The ethos of paternalism had always suffused Conservative thought. Where functions had to be transferred from individuals to the state, as in wartime, they were not frightened to extend the power of central authority. One element in the Conservative frame of mind was always the demand for 'strong' or 'firm' government. By this was meant not just the maintenance of social order, but also that government be conducted upon clear and consistent lines.

Conservatism had first emerged in response to the threat to property and the tyranny of the French Revolution; in the early twentieth century it was refurbished to tackle the similar twin dangers posed by 'Socialism' (**75**). The term was used not just to describe the aims of the emerging Labour Party but also to highlight the nature of all collectivist action, and so was applied to the policies of the Liberal governments of 1905–15 as well. In Conservative eyes Socialism would lead to the despotism of the mass over the propertied, impoverishing the latter without benefiting the former; Socialists prized loyalty to class above the national interest, and social antagonism was made an end in itself. The close regulation and loss of freedom which Socialism entailed were corrupting of personal and moral responsibility, eroding the natural self-reliance of individuals (**80**). Thus Socialism would directly and indirectly inhibit economic activity, lead to an upwards spiral of taxation and deficit and ultimately bring about national bankruptcy. Conservatives had no trouble in developing an extensive critique of Socialism, seizing adroitly upon any error or excess by its proponents. Much of this struck a chord with the temperament of 'natural conservatives', with the self-interest of the propertied upper classes, and with the social insecurity of the suburban lower-middle class. But in the age of 'democracy' their number was not enough to hold the line without substantial re-inforcement from the working class. Conservatives doubted that this could be obtained by merely negative, anti-Socialist rhetoric. Some feared that too narrow a *'laissez-faire'* attitude to government would drive that Conservative hero, the patriotic working man, into the arms of the agitators and revolutionaries. Yet Conservatives intent upon the preservation of existing society could hardly compete with Socialism in an auction of material promises. Between the wars, Conservatives were also anxious about their inability to match what they perceived to be the constant commitment and energy of Labour Party activists, who were believed to be spreading the word of Socialism in their neighbourhoods with untiring missionary zeal. Fear and ignorance meant that the scale and effectiveness of this was much overrated, but it was a powerful stimulus to Conservative politics, from the local branches through the constituency MP to the party leader. A positive gospel was therefore needed as an alternative to Socialism, and many hoped and believed that Tariff Reform and its accompanying vision of imperial greatness would fill this need.

British Conservatives were fortunate in that the ideas of their opponents could so often be portrayed as being of foreign origin and thereby alien, inferior, and unsuitable for any patriot. This was the case from Rousseau, the *Philosophes*, Comte and Mazzini to the revolutionary nostrums of Marx, Lenin and Fascism. Liberalism, and still more Socialism, could be depicted as Continental in inspiration and be tarred with the failings of their least attractive European parallels. Harold Begbie in *The Conservative Mind*, written under a pseudonym in 1925, was typical in asserting that 'modern Socialism is a mushroom forced by Russian atheism on the dunghill of German economics'. British Conservatism was insular and isolationist in its own outlook. It had very little contact with or fellow feeling for the parties of the right abroad, disliking the close links most of these had both to industry and to the Catholic Church.

The role of Conservatism

British Conservatism was 'an attempt to make intelligible what has been done and what is being done' (**4**). This twin function meant that a large measure of adaptability accompanied rather than contradicted the emphasis upon tradition. The existing order would not have come about had it not great merit, and so it should be upheld against change; but once conceded, most reforms proved not to have the apocalyptic consequences which Conservatives had feared. Instead, they soon become an inextricable part of the matrix of society, whilst the focus of struggle moved away to other issues and other fronts. It has been suggested that for this reason 'Conservative thought moves in self-fulfilling circles' (**77**). It was rarely reactionary, and focused primarily upon conserving the present. Conservative principles were not abstractions but tools, which were used for practical ends. The attitudes, prejudices and imagery of Conservatism were employed to prevent a polarisation of class against class and to secure the legitimacy of hierarchical authority. They sought to maintain a national identity, pride and purpose which would make Britain strong in time of peace and united in war or crisis; they could be directed both to limit and to excuse action taken by the state. Finally, they made a crucial contribution to attracting the support which the party needed in order to win power.

The Conservative outlook was transmitted to a wider public by several means. The first of these was the speeches of leading figures, heard either directly at the mass meetings which were the mainstay of political campaigning until the 1950s, or by radio broadcast from the early 1920s. Second was the role of the popular mass-circulation press: political reporting in these newspapers was not as extensive as in the 'quality' titles, but presentation and message were constant enough to have some influence. Most people choose to purchase the newspaper which they find congenial, and thus the press reinforces their views rather than changing or creating them. Nevertheless, the fact that after the decline of the Liberal press in the 1920s almost every popular newspaper was a clear if sometimes fractious supporter of the Conservatives must have helped to shape the general atmosphere of what was possible or plausible. Third, the direct dissemination of the party's own literature played its part. Posters, leaflets and publications contained many resonant images in both language and visual depiction, especially in cartoons. Subtlety was discarded in order to achieve an impact at a single glance, and there was a common currency of crude stereotypes. Emblems of national unity such as the flag, Britannia, and the plain yeoman figure of John Bull were set against the vagabond agitator behind whom stood sinister, dirty, bearded Bolsheviks with revolvers stuck in their belts. Conservatives could draw upon a rich array of such simple slogans and clichés and thereby exploit the truths of 'conventional wisdom', almost all of which were redolent of low expectations and the comfort provided by conformity (**145**).

As a whole, the simultaneous cohesion and adaptability of Conservative attitudes gave the party two great benefits. The first was a feeling of distinction from the other political groups. Whilst there was migration into the ranks of Conservatism between the 1880s and 1950s, there was no significant loss of Conservative supporters to any other movement. Occasional protests were registered by apathy on the part of active members and by abstention on the part of voters, but both returned to the fold when their needs were met or when other concerns supplanted them. The second advantage was an underlying unity of purpose which helped to keep the party together and which enabled it to recover from dissension without suffering serious damage. Through unspoken assumptions rather than inquiry and debate, Conservatives were generally agreed on what should in essence be conserved. However, this does not mean they agreed upon the details, nor upon what tactics of resistance, reform, compromise or concession should be employed. It is this which tended to cause the apparently impressive unity and consensus of resistance to fray in defeat or under sustained pressure; when it did so, the unravelling could be rapid and very unpredictable. Throughout the period, reference was often made to 'Conservative principles' without any further definition; this was because Conservatives knew and understood, especially on an emotional level, what was meant, and responded or judged accordingly. Conservatism was not required to remain a constant catechism; it reacted to the events and society in which it existed, varying as it adjusted to 'the colouration of time and place' (**81**). Its values and traditions reflected those of the social groups which supported the Conservative Party. Together these created Conservative policies and priorities, with the only constraints being the party leaders' acceptance that politics were 'the art of the possible' and the constant distraction of chance and circumstance.

Part Two: Conservative Politics

4   The Edwardian Crisis, 1902–14

Balfour's leadership

When the 3rd Marquis of Salisbury retired from the premiership due to age and ill-health in July 1902, his coalition ministry of Conservatives and their minority wing of Liberal Unionist allies had been in office for seven years and had won two consecutive general elections. Despite the long period of difficulty which the Conservatives had endured in the mid-nineteenth century, by 1902 they had become accustomed to regarding themselves as the natural party of government. The belief that it was their duty and destiny to guard the fortunes of the most extensive empire the world had ever seen meant that they were ill-equipped to cope with the problems of the next twelve years. These threatened to tear the party to pieces or leave it beached upon the sterile shores of extremism, once more a permanent minority party. Neither the survival of the Conservative Party nor its successful competition for power should be taken for granted, for there were points between 1902 and 1951 when it might as easily have fragmented or collapsed.

Although there were already underlying signs of strain (**14**), in July 1902 these crises were still to come, and the succession to the premiership of Salisbury's nephew, Arthur James Balfour, was expected and uncontested. There were only two other figures of sufficient weight to be considered, but both were too old and, as Liberal Unionists, effectively out of the running for the Conservative leadership (the formal merger did not take place until 1912). They were the 8th Duke of Devonshire, the widely respected senior figure in the Liberal Unionist revolt against Gladstone, and the radical Joseph Chamberlain. The latter was a forceful and inventive politician, one of the rare few whose initiatives 'made the political weather'; he was the most powerful member of the Cabinet after Balfour himself. The new Prime Minister had many talents: a searching intellect which he exercised by writing works of serious philosophy, a forensic superiority in debate in the House of

Commons, and an inner ruthlessness. Balfour was deeply concerned about the country's international isolation and the modernisation of the army and navy (**42**). He had overseen the passage of the 1902 Education Act shortly before becoming Prime Minister, and in the following year created the basis of the modern Cabinet Office, the Committee of Imperial Defence. To remain in office long enough to ensure the permanence of these measures – the often forgotten achievements of an otherwise ill-starred premiership – Balfour was prepared to make many sacrifices, and this explains his strategy during the period 1903–5. Some of Balfour's problems during his tenure of the party leadership stemmed from his own character. A lifelong bachelor, cool, detached and languidly superior, he never entirely shook off the impression that there was something feline or feminine in his nature, and epithets and cartoons constantly depicted him as an old maid. Balfour was aloof and subtle, and neither his personality nor his style of politics were capable of giving an inspirational lead when the party found itself facing division and defeat. Time and again between 1902 and 1911 Balfour was to disappoint the hopes of his followers for a clear and simple lead on policy or even, in 1911, on tactics. He remained leader for as long as he did partly due to the tradition of loyalty, and partly because the possible alternatives seemed to be vastly his inferior in ability [**doc. 8**].

Balfour's succession was not a matter of nepotism – he had proved himself as leader in the Commons since 1891 – but too much else about his ministry had that appearance. His brother and several cousins held ministerial office, an inevitable result of the narrow social base of inter-married aristocratic families from which the leadership was drawn. This was not a problem when all went well but made an easy target when it did not, and hence the jibes about the 'Hotel Cecil' (**53**). The party suffered from a lack of front-bench talent throughout the Edwardian era, in particular after 1906. Most of the generation of leaders who had dominated the scene since the 1880s retired from active politics along with Salisbury between 1900 and 1906. This natural process was given an unnatural impetus by the divisions over tariff reform in 1903, for the free-trade minority included several senior figures and elder statesmen. The election defeat of 1906 removed a large number of front-benchers from the House of Commons and interrupted or ended the careers of many of the junior ministers from whom the next generation of leaders would normally have emerged. The severity of the reverse also affected the ex-ministers who survived the landslide, and their lack of energy and slack attendance in the House were a matter of constant complaint between 1906 and 1912; this aloofness and amateurism also undermined the morale of the backbenchers (**90, 181**). The party was unlucky in the incidence of early deaths amongst its remaining leaders during these years. To the unexpected loss of Arnold-Forster, Percy, Wyndham and Lyttlelton could be added Joseph Chamberlain, a permanent invalid after his stroke in July 1906. Several of the most experienced and effective ministers who remained in the shadow cabinet, such as Lansdowne, Selborne, Curzon, Milner and Derby, were removed from the immediate fray because they were members of the House of Lords. These factors made Balfour's pre-eminence in the House of Commons seem all the greater, perhaps excessively so. They also explain why Andrew Bonar Law, first elected in 1900 and a junior minister in 1902–5, and F.E. Smith, who made a tremendous impact with his maiden speech in 1906, were able to rise so swiftly to the top of the party between 1906 and 1911.

Tariff reform

The Conservative Party's success between 1886 and 1900 derived partly from the temporary factors of Conservative organisational strength and Liberal apathy and disunity. The advantage of being the party in office meant that the Conservatives were able to determine the timing of almost all of the elections in this period. Their aim was to limit the turnout of working-class voters. In rural areas, the Conservative position was defended by holding the election at harvest time, when it was difficult for agricultural labourers to go to the poll. At the same time the borough electorate diminished as the annual register of electors, based upon claims made nearly eighteen months before, approached the end of its term. The tenant and lodger franchises which covered most working-class electors laid down that a change of abode – even within the same constituency – meant disqualification until a fresh register was compiled. For that reason, the much greater mobility of the working class reduced the proportion of 'the lower classes of citizen' actually voting (**96**).

These factors had worked in favour of the Conservatives up to 1900, but during the following five years changes which were to undermine their position appeared simultaneously and with little warning. These were first an anti-Conservative popular reaction, second a revival of the Liberal Party, and finally the emergence of a third party, Labour, which, although small in number, enabled the Liberals to mobilise vital working-class support (**86**). Long-term economic and social changes played a part in these developments, but they were also the result of the short-term difficulties which the Balfour ministry encountered. Critically, several of these were in the very areas of imperial, defence and Irish policy in which the Unionists claimed a special competence. There were problems over army reforms, over military policy in India, and over Ireland, where the responsible minister, Wyndham, was forced to resign after appearing to endorse a scheme which to suspicious Unionist eyes seemed to be a stepping-stone to Home Rule. Another imperial issue which caused much domestic outcry was the use of indentured labourers from the Far East, 'Chinese slavery', to work in the reconstruction of South Africa after the Boer War. As well as the indignation aroused by their living and working conditions, the issue symbolised for much working-class opinion a feeling of exclusion from the benefits of empire which had been so trumpeted during the war. This became linked to the view that the Conservatives were hostile to trade unionism, due to the government's refusal to restore the privileges undermined by the Taff Vale case of 1901. Chinese labour also combined with two other issues to outrage Nonconformity at the very time when its last great revival was taking place in 1904–5. Most damaging was the reaction to the religious provisions of the Education Act of 1902, but the Licensing Act of 1904 also revitalised another great Liberal cause. The alienation of Nonconformity stimulated the revival of the Liberals and led to the defection of Liberal Unionist supporters.

The Unionists might have overcome their difficulties had they not been distracted and divided by the greatest problem of them all: the crusade for tariff reform launched by Joseph Chamberlain in 1903. This became a central theme of Conservative politics for the next three decades, and was to lead to four election defeats before final success in 1931. Tariff reform was offered as the solution to the problems which Britain and the Unionist government faced at the beginning of the twentieth century. The domestic weaknesses and international isolation which were revealed by the Boer War, together with the economic advance of Germany and the United States, both from behind the shelter of protective tariff barriers, led to a crisis of confidence in governing circles. Schemes of 'national efficiency', of 'social-imperialism', of radical realignments and of collectivist reforms, were all in the air between 1900 and 1906 and shaped the ideas of both the New Liberalism and tariff reform (**113**). In 1895 Chamberlain had chosen to go to the Colonial Office, and although diverted by the Boer War he had consistently sought some means of bringing the colonies of settlement, the dominions, into a closer partnership with the mother country, to their mutual benefit. He understood that sentiment alone was not enough, and that the dominions were developing into separate nations and building up their own manufacturing base behind protective barriers. An economic initiative was needed to counter the centrifugal forces in the empire, and the colonial premiers made clear that only a scheme of reciprocal preference would be acceptable (**116**). Existing colonial tariffs would be reduced or removed in the case of British manufacturing exports, and in return the mother country would offer a protected market for colonial produce [**doc. 3**].

There were two great political problems in this. Britain had been the exemplar of free-trade economics since the 1840s and so would first have to impose tariff duties on all incoming goods before being able to lower them for the dominions. As the latter were still primarily agricultural exporters, this would mean not just tariffs on manufactured goods but also on raw materials and – most sensitive of all – on cheap food imports. The unavoidable implication was that this would raise the cost of staple foodstuffs such as wheat and meat, and so press heavily and unfairly upon the urban working-class household. This was tariff reform's most vulnerable point, for it was easy for opponents to hark back to the cries of the 1840s and arouse fears of 'stomach taxes'. The bogey of 'dear food', supported by alarming parallels with the 'black bread and horse-meat' diet of the German working class, gave the enemies of tariff reform a simple, negative but highly effective weapon which could constantly be used against it. However, for the staunchest tariff reformers, including Chamberlain himself, imperial preference was the cardinal aspect of the policy. The food taxes which it required could not be jettisoned on the narrow pragmatic grounds of their electoral unpopularity. Far from questioning its practicality or intrinsic merits, tariff reformers were convinced that it was timid and defensive presentations of the policy which were to blame for its rejection. The diametrically opposite conclusions which different elements in the party drew from the same electoral evidence was a problem throughout this era [**doc. 5**]. Free-fooders and Balfourite moderates had little hesitation in attributing the party's defeats to the tariff policy and above all to food taxes, and feared that in their monomania and doctrinal rigidity the protectionists would sacrifice the Church, the Union and the constitution. On the other hand, the tariff reformers discerned a pattern whereby those who campaigned positively as 'whole-hoggers', committed to the full tariff programme, appeared to be more successful and so increased as a proportion of the parliamentary party. In their eyes this proved that the policy could be an asset rather than a liability, if only the party was united behind it and led with boldness and resolution. This feeling led them to view the caution of Balfour and the Central Office as the first and greatest danger and gave the edge to the factional struggles of 1903–13. Tariff reform was the product of 'radical Unionism', and its opponents within the party were defending not just free trade but a traditional type of Conservatism against collectivism, materialism and class antagonism.

The imperial aspect of the tariff policy made the greatest appeal to Unionist idealism, but the future of the empire was not the only vital issue which it addressed. It could fulfil other functions, the first of which was the protection of domestic industries from all external competition. This did not require the inclusion of agriculture, and hence food taxes could be avoided. The prosperity of an industry was a matter of interest not only to its leaders but also to the workers whose livelihood depended upon it. In this way tariff reform could be presented as being in the best interests of the urban working class, and candidates often campaigned under the slogan of 'work and wages'. From the start, Chamberlain sought to demonstrate that the increased cost of food would be more than outweighed by the advantages of employment and prosperity which tariffs would bring. By the turn of the century most Conservatives believed that the practical limits of direct taxation had been reached and that the country faced a financial impasse. Tariff reform offered a solution through increased indirect taxation, and it was on these lines that the fiscal battle was fought between Unionists and Liberals up to 1914. Under the seductive cry that the foreigner would pay, the tariff could provide the revenue to finance social reforms such as old-age pensions, promised by Chamberlain himself since 1895 but delayed due to the cost of the Boer War. Tariff reform was intended to provide the working class with an economic motive for voting Conservative; it was also a gospel to be preached, a crusade through which the imagination of the people could be caught. It would therefore counter both the

41

material and idealistic appeals of 'Socialism' [**doc. 4**]. Finally, tariff reform was designed to tackle the problems the Unionist government faced after 1902, to recover lost popularity and to regain the initiative. The Irish question had been in abeyance since 1895 and a new positive and inspirational focus was required. 'It was an essential attribute of tariff reform that it was a single policy to solve a multitude of problems, and that it could respond to changing circumstances by changes of emphasis' (113). It had a potent appeal to both the pockets and the hearts of the party's natural constituency, and despite the disunity and defeats which resulted it was to retain a powerful hold upon the Conservative psyche for years to come.

Divisions and defeats

The tariff-reform crisis began with the registration duty on imported corn imposed in the 1902 budget, Sir Michael Hicks-Beach's last before retiring. Chamberlain wanted to use this as the first step towards imperial preference but was thwarted by the new Chancellor, C.T. Ritchie, who threatened to resign before presenting his first budget if he was not allowed to repeal the duty and restore free trade. However, the dogmatism with which Ritchie announced this in the 1903 budget speech, and the formation around him of a free-trade clique in the Cabinet, alienated Balfour. The rifts within the ministry became still more apparent when Chamberlain spoke publicly in favour of preference at Birmingham on 15 May 1903 [**doc. 3**]. It was the manner of this speech rather than its content which caused a sensation, but in the Commons on 22 and 28 May Chamberlain unfolded a more radical programme. During the following three years, by his boldness and persistence Chamberlain succeeded in his aim of making tariff reform 'the great question of the future, the one on which party divisions will ultimately settle themselves' (93). However, the first divisions to appear were not between the parties but within the Unionist ranks. Within a few weeks of Chamberlain's speech the backbench supporters of each faction had established their own pressure groups, destroying the unity of the parliamentary party. The Unionist Free Food League emerged first on 13 July: a collection of elderly chiefs with too few Indians, it was always outnumbered and on the defensive. Far wealthier and more powerful was the Tariff Reform League, formed on 21 July with Chamberlain's unofficial blessing to carry the message of preference and convert the country.

In this it failed, but within the Unionist Party tariff reform secured the adherence of many MPs and swept the rank and file in 1903–5. In May 1904 Chamberlain ousted Devonshire from the presidency of the Liberal Unionist Association, which from then on acted as a tariff-reform caucus. Still more effective was the Tariff Reform League, which spread rapidly to total nearly 300 constituency branches by 1906. Under these pressures many MPs began to shift their stance and at least appear to lean in the Chamberlainite direction. This left the position of the free-fooders still more exposed, and the energy and passion of the younger imperialists such as Amery and Page Croft were mobilised to capture their local associations or to threaten them with rival tariff-reform candidates. Between 1903 and 1910 the Unionist free-traders suffered erosion from all sides (**103, 97**). Some of the most determined, such as the young Winston Churchill, crossed the floor to join the Liberal Party; at the other end of the spectrum some suppressed their views out of party loyalty or the fear of deselection. Many free-fooders decided to stand down; others were hounded out by local hostility fanned by Tariff Reform League branches (**87**). After 1906 those who still remained were the target of further attacks, orchestrated by a secretive group of younger tariff reformers known as the Confederates (**112**). By 1910 there was hardly a single openly free-trade Unionist MP left, but this apparent unanimity did not mean that the parliamentary party had all become genuine converts to the 'whole-hogger' cause.

Balfour could do little to halt the advance of tariff reform amongst the lower ranks, but he was determined to try to hold his party together at the top. On 13 August 1903 he tried to secure Cabinet unity behind a compromise policy of 'retaliation' in a memorandum published as *Economic Notes on Insular Free Trade*. Later summarised on 'a half-sheet of notepaper', this middle way became the official policy until after the 1906 election and provided an umbrella under which the pragmatic moderates could shelter. Although most of the Cabinet adhered to Balfour's neutral position, the dissension of the free-traders was clear. At the same time Chamberlain decided to leave the Cabinet in order to lead the tariff campaign in the country; his departure was amicably but privately arranged with Balfour. This gave the Prime Minister room to manoeuvre, and at the next Cabinet on 14 September 1903 he ruthlessly purged Ritchie and two other free-trade ministers, whilst seeking to retain the respected figurehead of the Duke of Devonshire. The tactical skill of Balfour's coup has attracted historical admiration (**95**), but in fact it succeeded neither in the long term nor the short term. His conscience assailed by the sacked free-traders, Devonshire used the pretext of Balfour's 'retaliationist' speech at the National Union conference at Sheffield on 1 October to resign as well. Between 1903 and 1905 Balfour tried to prevent the wounds from deepening by refusing to discuss the tariff issue. The party ducked debates moved by the Liberals, but at the expense of its self-respect and prestige; this period permanently damaged Balfour's reputation. It was marked by a string of by-election defeats, a paralysis of command, a visible decay, and internecine warfare at local level. The capture of the party from below by the tariff reformers also meant that it was only a matter of time before this strategy became bankrupt. Balfour's decision to resign as Prime Minister on 4 December 1905 directly followed Chamberlain's capture of the National Union conference and his attempts to force the adoption of tariff reform as official policy. The timing of the resignation was also influenced by hopes of exploiting Liberal disagreements, but these evaporated and Sir Henry Campbell-Bannerman had no difficulty in forming a powerful ministry. Parliament was then dissolved, and the Conservatives fought the general election of January 1906 as the opposition party. Despite their many problems the Unionist vote held steady or even rose slightly, and losses were due more to the still greater increases in the Liberal poll. However, in practical terms the outcome was catastrophic, with only 157 Unionist MPs returned to face 400 Liberals, 83 Irish Nationalists and 30 of the newly formed Labour Party.

The defeat not only drastically reduced the size of the parliamentary party but also changed the balance within it. An estimate published by *The Times* on 30 January 1906 suggested that 109 MPs were tariff reformers, with the Balfourites reduced to 32 and the free-fooders to 11, and 5 unclassified. To contemporaries this clearly gave Chamberlain the whip hand, although a more searching classification by historians has indicated that his supporters numbered 79 at the most, and that as many as 31 free-traders still survived (**85**). Chamberlain also held another ace: with Balfour temporarily out of the House after losing his own seat and other leading ministers also defeated, there was no credible alternative to Chamberlain as acting-leader of the opposition when the new session opened – with all that this implied for the definition of policy and even for the permanent leadership. Against this threat-ening background Chamberlain demanded that a party meeting be convened at the start of the new session to discuss policy, organ-isation and the acting-leadership. The first fortnight of February saw a period of tense and intense negotiation (**93, 88**). Balfour was determined not to surrender the leader's authority over policy to the party meeting, or his control over the Central Office to the National Union. To maintain these he was willing to advance on policy, especially as to do so would now aid rather than diminish party unity, and to make some concessions on reorganisation. Chamberlain was also restrained by the need not to seem disloyal and by awareness of the damage that an open confrontation would do, and so the eventual result was a compromise. The meeting was rendered a mere formality by a published exchange between Chamberlain and Balfour on the day before, 14 February 1906, ironically named the 'Valentine letters'. In these Balfour declared that tariff reform was 'the first constructive work of the Unionist Party'. Although vague and qualified afterwards, the Valentine letters represented a marked advance in Balfour's official position. The compact was 'a major doctrinal triumph' for the tariff reformers, and accepted as such by Chamberlain (**85, 19**). How-ever, his ascendancy was cut short on 11 July 1906 when he suffered a paralytic stroke. Chamberlain's condition was kept secret by his family and for many months there was uncertainty as to whether he could return to active politics, but by 1908 it was clear that this was impossible and his influence was greatly dimin-ished. The leadership of the tariff-reform movement devolved upon his son Austen, Chancellor of the Exchequer from 1903 to 1905, who lacked the forcefulness and authority of his father.

Balfour's strategy in opposition was to concentrate upon attack-ing specific Liberal measures, especially where they lacked wide-spread popular appeal, and to avoid providing a target in return by promulgating the detailed programme which the 'whole-hoggers' constantly sought. With the tariff-reform camp in confusion, Balfour was able to pursue this strategy without challenge over the Education Bill during the remainder of 1906. However, by the beginning of 1907 his neglect of tariffs was threatening to provoke a revolt, and so at Hull on 1 February he reaffirmed the 'Valentine' policy. Influenced by the economist W.A.S. Hewins and the opinions voiced at the Colonial conference of April–May 1907, Balfour gave tariff reform greater prominence in two key state-ments later that year at the Albert Hall and at the conference of the National Union in Birmingham. The latter declaration defined the official position until 1910 and was used not only by the 'whole-hoggers' but also by the Central Office as the litmus test of loyalty. The Chief Whip, Acland-Hood, was incapable of subtlety, and 'under his direction most of Balfour's speeches were interpreted with the qualifications left out' (**85**). After 1906 the leader and Central Office became increasingly impatient with the dissidence of the free-traders and refused to shield them from attack. Yet to the tariff reformers every 'forward' move of Balfour's seemed reluctant and coerced, and they came to regard him as a hindrance and not a help. In 1906–11 the atmosphere in Unionist politics was an unhealthy mixture of factionalism and distrust, with the moderates resentful of 'whole-hogger' tactics and the free-fooders in despair. Although the tariff reformers seemed to be in the ascendant, they felt themselves engaged in a constant struggle to keep their policy from adulteration.

In 1908 Balfour concentrated the party's fire against the Liberals' Licensing Bill. The massive Unionist majority in the House of Lords was used to thwart this and a range of other measures between 1906 and 1909 for which it was argued the government had no constitutional mandate (**105**). When the Liberal Chancellor of the Exchequer, Lloyd George, ingeniously revived these Bills by incorporating their financial provisions into his first budget in 1909, the Conservative reaction was that such blatant 'tacking' abnegated the convention that the upper House could not amend a budget. Unionists had long argued that the House of Lords had the right and duty to block reforms which had not been endorsed at an election and so force their reference back to the people. To meet the cost of the old-age pensions introduced in 1908 and the naval race with Germany, Lloyd George was also proposing radical extensions of direct taxation carefully targeted upon the upper rather than the middle class. In this way the 'People's Budget' would shatter the Unionist claim that the limit of free-trade finance had been reached and that only tariffs could bridge the deficit and provide social reform and security (**100**). Responding to the challenge, Balfour adopted tariff reform as the party's positive alternative to the 'Socialism' of the budget [**doc. 4**]. In this he was followed by a remarkably united party, for even the strongest Unionist free-traders accepted that the mirage of a centre ground had vanished and that protection was the lesser of the two evils before them (**113**).

The opposition in the Commons was revitalised, and for five

months the Finance Bill was resisted line by line. A Budget Protest League under the leading front-bencher, Walter Long, carried the campaign to the country. By the autumn it was clear that permitting the passage of the budget was a worse danger than rejecting it. Balfour and the leader of the party in the House of Lords, the Marquess of Lansdowne, were aware of the risks which they were taking and of the likelihood of electoral defeat, but accepted that the logic of their position required rejection [**doc. 6**]. On 30 November 1909 the House of Lords threw out the budget by 350 to 75 and a general election followed, with polling in January 1910, giving the government the advantage of a fresh register. During the campaign, tariff reform became swamped by the class issue of aristocratic privilege and the cry of 'peers versus people'. The imperial side of the policy was overshadowed by its domestic role in raising revenue without hitting the propertied with higher taxation: this seemed to fuse with the self-interest of the landowners and peers, and the defence of vested interests at the expense of the poor. The Unionists had not developed a 'constructive' social policy with which to complement the protectionist aspect of tariff reform, for Balfour had neglected and resisted this, and so they had little to offer urban working-class voters to counter the appeal of the budget (**89**). Turnout in the election and the total Unionist vote both reached record levels, and the party recovered many of the seats in central and southern England which had been lost in 1906. But this was not enough to dislodge the Liberals from office, and the 273 Unionists faced a bloc of 275 Liberals, 82 Irish Nationalists and 40 Labour MPs.

The constitutional crisis

After the election the 'People's Budget' was passed without any further resistance. The results left the reform of the House of Lords at the top of the agenda whilst making the Liberals dependent on Irish support. This produced a crisis within the ministry in April which tantalisingly held out the possibility of its collapse, but the Cabinet secured Irish agreement for the tackling of the Lords first as the prelude to the introduction of a Home Rule Bill. From this point onwards the alliance of Liberals, Irish and Labour was to prove unshakeable, and this led to mounting Unionist frustration amidst claims that the government was being maintained in office by a corrupt, 'log-rolling', unnatural alliance. This was the background to the constitutional crisis of 1910–14, and explains the passion and bitterness which infused not only the Unionist rank and file but also the leadership.

In the early months of 1910 the Lords debated eleventh-hour plans for their own reform, but there was little consensus and still less conviction about this. The Liberal Cabinet after some hesitation determined on the simplest and most effective course: to limit the upper House to a suspensory veto of no more than two years. However, the Lords would need to be coerced into passing this, and the creation of several hundred Liberal peers might ultimately be necessary. This depended upon the use of the royal prerogative and on the exact nature of the monarch's undertakings to the government; it would almost certainly require another general election fought specifically on the issue of the powers of the House of Lords. The death of Edward VII in May 1910 and the succession of the inexperienced George V led to attempts to find a compromise in the 'truce of God' conference attended by delegations of four Liberal and four Unionist leaders. These talks occupied the summer months but foundered on the Unionist demand that the limitation of the veto should not apply to a category of 'constitutional' bills which clearly would include Home Rule. Unionist leaders did not regret the abandonment of the conference on 10 November, for any deal would have been difficult to sell to the rank and file. George V was pressured by his ministers to give private guarantees to create peers if required after a further general election, and polling took place in December 1910. Conservatives were under no illusions as to what was at stake in this contest: the ancient constitution which they venerated and the interests which it protected would all face imminent radical attack once the shield of the Lords was broken. In January 1910 the party had fought on the full tariff programme and failed to win the day: although Austen Chamberlain and the ardent spirits disagreed [**doc. 5**], many Unionists drew the conclusion that tariff reform was an electoral liability. With Home Rule now looming large upon the political horizon, moderate tariff reformers began to back away from the unpopular and vulnerable commitment to food taxes. As the campaign progressed, Balfour received a stream of pleas to drop food taxes from candidates in marginal seats, especially in the key region of Lancashire which was to poll on the first day of voting and where free-trade sentiment remained strong. Compromise was also urged by leading tariff reformers such as the editor J.L. Garvin, F.E. Smith and, crucially, Bonar Law, who was standing in the highly symbolic commercial district of

Manchester North-west as the standard-bearer of tariff reform. Swift action was essential and, consulting only Lansdowne, on 29 November 1910 at the Albert Hall Balfour made the offer to submit tariff reform to a referendum if the Liberals would agree to do likewise with Home Rule. However, the stratagem did not have the desired effect: although a number of seats changed hands in the December 1910 general election, they cancelled each other out and left the balance of forces almost unchanged. The referendum was a risky initiative and its failure left the leader's position exposed, confirming the feeling that Balfour was both too autocratic and too pragmatic. Crucially it undermined shadow-cabinet unity and 'reinforced the tendency of his colleagues to act on their own initiative' (**94**).

The session of 1911 was marked by disunity, seething unrest, and a party leadership which once again appeared indecisive and ineffective, compromising basic principles without gaining any compensating advantage. It was dominated by the struggle over the Parliament Bill, which came before the upper House for the final confrontation in July. Only at this point was the royal pledge to create peers if necessary revealed by the government. Passions were running as high as the soaring heat-wave: on 24 July Asquith was howled down by Unionist backbenchers in the Commons and the sitting was suspended in chaos. Events had acquired their own momentum and many Unionists in both houses were committed to resistance and to 'die in the last ditch' if need be [**doc. 7**]. Forcing a mass creation of Liberal peers would have been emotionally satisfying, but counter-productive. It would not only have undermined the social exclusivity of the peerage but also permitted the Liberals to pass a raft of measures attacking Conservative interests: licensing, education, land, plural voting, the Church, and so on. Accordingly, those who accepted the need to bow to the inevitable and preserve the Unionist dominance in an upper chamber which would retain at least some powers of delay, the 'hedgers', narrowly carried the day at the shadow-cabinet meeting of 21 July 1911. On 24 July Lansdowne issued a circular to peers advising abstention in the final vote; Balfour endorsed this two days later in an open letter in *The Times*. However, the 'ditchers' were beyond restraint: their defiance was not a coherent policy but an expression of emotion, not only against the Liberal Bill but also against Balfour's style of leadership and the morass into which it seemed to have led: the attraction of a bold unequivocal stance, however futile, was too great for many MPs and peers (**92**). The 'ditcher' rally organised for 26 July in the shape of a dinner in honour of the former Lord Chancellor Halsbury assumed the appearance of a revolt, and ominously took more permanent form with the creation of a 'Halsbury Club'. Numbers were uncertain, but it seemed probable that the 'diehard' peers voting against the Bill might be sufficient to defeat the government supporters voting for it. As a result, in the final division on 10 August the Unionists split three ways: the majority followed Lansdowne into sullen abstention, whilst 114 'ditchers' entered the hostile lobby. The Bill was only passed because the 37 peers of the 'Judas group' were persuaded by the Unionist leaders to vote with the Liberals and avoid a mass creation (**109, 115**).

This humiliating shambles led directly to Balfour's decision a few weeks later to quit a leadership which he no longer felt served a useful purpose. The main factor in this was continued disunity in the parliamentary party and amongst its leaders, and not the public campaign under the slogan 'BMG' (Balfour must go) instigated by the marginal figure of Leo Maxse, editor of the 'diehard' *National Review*. After Balfour's announcement on 8 November, the party in the House of Commons was faced with the likelihood of still further rifts over the selection of his successor. As the party meeting summoned for the 13th approached, it became clear that neither of the two main candidates, Austen Chamberlain and Walter Long, could muster a majority, and, still worse, that the supporters of the one would not loyally serve under the other. Chamberlain was the abler and stronger candidate, but he symbolised the ascendancy of 'radical Unionism' and of food taxes, and there was resentment over his role in the Halsbury Club and apparent disloyalty to Balfour. Long, who was a country gentlemen and a moderate on tariff reform, had the support of the bulk of the MPs who sat for county divisions, but of none of the front bench, who considered him to lack competence and reliability. The resolution was unexpected, but proved unexpectedly satisfactory. At Austen Chamberlain's initial suggestion the two front-runners agreed to stand aside in favour of the outsider third candidate, Bonar Law, who was then elected unopposed.

Bonar Law was to prove much more effective than Balfour at uniting, invigorating and modernising the party: his leadership has been seen as crucial in restoring its confidence and morale and in putting its feet on the road to power (**6**). There is much truth in this, but renewed trouble over tariff reform nearly ended Bonar Law's tenure after only a year. In April 1912 the shadow cabinet decided to drop the referendum pledge, for the Liberals had not responded and were now bringing in a Home Rule Bill. There was much hesitancy, and the return to an overt food-tax policy was not made public until speeches given by Lansdowne and Law in November and December. These at once provoked a revolt. The same pressures which had led to the referendum pledge of December 1910 now also combined to force the abandonment of the food taxes: the determined opposition of the pragmatists and moderates on electoral grounds, and the overriding priority of the defence of the Union and the established interests for which the party stood. The events of December 1912 to January 1913 saw the triumph of 'conservative' protectionism over the 'radical Unionism' of the 'constructive' policy (**113**). Bonar Law initially had made his reputation as 'whole-hogger', but under pressure from all sides, and in particular a threat of direct repudiation by the Lancashire division of the National Union [**doc. 9**], he was forced to reverse his stance and acquiesce in the emasculation of Joseph Chamberlain's great ideal. Both Law and Lansdowne felt that having done so they must resign, but there were no suitable replacements for either. They were pressed to remain by a petition which was signed by almost every Unionist MP, and after a show of reluctance agreed to carry on. In one respect this was a step forward: after a decade of strife, the party had finally escaped from the electoral minefield of food taxes. But cutting out the heart of tariff reform also left a massive gap in Conservative social policy: the party developed nothing in its place to counter the appeal of the Liberal programme. It was symptomatic that the need was addressed not by the leadership but by an unofficial group, the Unionist Social Reform Committee, and that their radical proposals were negatively received (**104**).

Instead, all energies between 1912 and 1914 were focused upon the old battleground of Irish Home Rule. The Conservative opposition in the Commons sought to keep the government and its supporters under constant pressure and to put up a fight which would rally opinion in the country against the Bill. Dogged parliamentary resistance was enlivened by periodic attempts at catching the ministry out in a 'snap' division. So much legislative time was consumed that other damaging Liberal measures, such as the elimination of plural votes for business premises, had to be dropped. But however hard the opposition fought they could not prevent the Home Rule Bill from becoming law before the next general election, and the knowledge of this fact frustrated and enraged them. Their heartfelt convictions were, first, that the Liberals had secured no mandate for Home Rule in 1910 and, second, that, if offered the chance, the nation would not give such a mandate, especially if it implied the coercion of the Protestant North. Unionists also regarded the constitution as being 'in suspense', as the Parliament Act had been presented as a holding measure prior to a fundamental reconstitution and reform of the Lords. The government's attempt to proceed with organic change without first honouring this undertaking was regarded by many Unionists as justifying unconstitutional methods of opposition. Bonar Law believed that an election fought on the Irish issue would give the Unionists their best chance of recovering power: it was therefore necessary to force the Liberals to dissolve Parliament before Home Rule was passed. The obvious weakness of the measure was the vehement refusal of Ulster to be subordinated to a Catholic parliament in Dublin. It was for this reason that Bonar Law committed the party to the unlimited support of Ulster resistance. The strategy was one of brinkmanship: with the approval of his followers Bonar Law 'tied the party of order to the forces of disorder' so as to achieve 'a constitutional change in government by unconstitutional threats' (**110**). This path involved high risks, but, although uncompromising, Bonar Law was not reckless: his 'extremism' was planned and purposeful (**6**).

As the crisis deepened Bonar Law did not flinch, although the need at· least to appear reasonable led to participation in the 'secret' talks with Asquith of October–December 1913 and in the formal conference at Buckingham Palace on 21–24 July 1914. The Conservatives spurned the 'stay of execution' under which Ulster would remain outside the Bill for as much as six years, despite the fact that this would carry the matter over not one but two general elections. Their demand for permanent exclusion – the partition of Ireland – was unacceptable to the Nationalists and therefore to a Liberal government which depended upon their votes: it was at this point of impasse that the European crisis and war suddenly intervened at the end of July 1914. In their efforts to thwart Home Rule and force an election, the Unionists adopted unconstitutional language and considered unconstitutional methods [**doc. 10**]. To a large extent the party bound itself hand and foot to the Ulster cause. Unconditional support implicated it in the preparations there for armed defiance, with all the potential for bloody civil war which this implied. One of the party's leading figures, Sir Edward Carson, was prominently involved in the plan to establish an illegal provisional government in Belfast when Home Rule became law. Conservatives pressured the King to withhold the royal assent if there was no dissolution, whilst the leadership considered blocking in the Lords the annual Army Act which enforced military discipline. This would remove the government's means of forcing the implementation of Home Rule: the reluctance of the officer corps had already been underlined by the false alarm of the 'Curragh mutiny' in March 1914.

The violence of language, mood of frustration and tendency to faction of the Edwardian Unionist Party have led some historians to detect the existence of a 'crisis of Conservatism' and to identify the emergence of a 'radical right' (**102**). The two main strands were those of traditional paternalist Toryism, typified by Lord Willoughby de Broke, and the 'efficiency' of the social-imperialists, of whom Lord Milner was the leading exponent. Both elements contained a range of individuals whose ideas and emphases often substantially differed. Nevertheless, most subscribed to a common agenda which, beyond 'diehard' resistance to Liberal measures, included the strengthening of the army and navy, the introduction of compulsory national service for both military and moral reasons, 'whole-hog' tariff reform and anti-Socialism. It has been suggested that the 'radical right' showed traits akin to later fascism: they were 'xenophobic, demagogic and attracted to conspiracy theories' (**108**). There was an element of anti-Semitism in their constant denunciations of 'cosmopolitan finance' and the 'radical plutocracy', and the Marconi scandal of 1913 confirmed every prejudice. However, the distinctiveness and significance of the 'radical right' has been questioned: 'the salient characteristic of the Edwardian right was its confusion' (**114**). In fact, the larger element of traditionalist 'diehards' shaded into the party mainstream. Their rhetoric and methods stand out as more 'extreme', but this is not synonymous with being more 'radical': their immediate goals and long-term aims were the same. In this view it is the small group of Milnerites who were aberrant and largely isolated 'the "radical right" was all but swamped in a sea of traditional Conservatives defending traditional causes' (**114**).

Conservative politics in the Edwardian era of 1902–14 were marked by anxiety and frustration over the party's electoral position, dissatisfaction with its leadership, disputes over remedies, internal chaos and factionalism. One symptom of this fragmentation was the emergence of sectional pressure groups of a kind hitherto associated with the faddism of the Liberal frame of mind:

the tariff reformers were the most prominent of the 'plague of leagues' from which the Conservatives suffered (**87**). Yet, despite all these problems of leadership, policy and organisation, the party held together. It may have threatened to break up but never actually did so; its resilience has perhaps been underestimated. All that was needed for the restoration of unity and discipline was a cause which was both patriotic and popular. This was provided by the coming of the First World War, which at once pushed every other issue and dispute into the background.

5   War and Coalition, 1914–22

Patriotic opposition

The First World War had a dramatic impact upon politics in Britain. By the end of 1918 the electoral system had been fundamentally changed, and the fortunes of the four parties which were represented in Parliament in 1914 had been transformed. One of the first effects of the outbreak of hostilities abroad was the negotiation of a truce at home between the parties which allowed for the unopposed filling of by-election vacancies. The life of the existing House of Commons was also prolonged by periodic agreement, and so the general election which would have been due by December 1915 was postponed for the duration. Historians have differed over the hypothetical question of who would have won such an election if the war had not intervened. Those who regard a Liberal defeat as the most probable outcome have done so for two reasons, separate but not incompatible. The first focuses upon the internal health of the Liberal Party and the challenge from Labour, it being assumed that conflict between the two was inevitable and that the Liberals would have been the losers. Distinct from this is the suggestion that the Conservative Party had gained in strength since 1910 and could have won under its own steam (**6**). There is evidence to support both views, but in each case reservations emerge upon closer examination. The Conservatives had made a string of gains in by-elections since 1910, but many of these were due to the opposition vote being split between rival Liberal and Labour candidates. It was likely that such rivalry would be suppressed almost everywhere in a general election and that the Lib-Lab pact of 1903 would continue to operate as a highly effective anti-Conservative front. Conservative by-election gains were therefore as likely to evaporate as to form stepping-stones to victory. Nor can it be assumed that the municipal election advances which the Conservatives had made since 1906 would have translated into parliamentary seats. Whilst the vitality and unity of the party had been restored under Bonar Law's uncompromising leadership, this may have been at the expense of more moderate support and of the party's credibility as an alternative government. Since the reforms of 1911 the efficiency of the party organisation had greatly improved, but organisation alone cannot win elections unless a party can appeal outside its own normal body of supporters.

The great weakness of the Conservative Party in 1914 remained its lack of an attractive domestic policy. The 1913 compromise on tariff reform may have prevented internal strife, but it lacked credibility and still left the party open to attack as advocating food taxes, eventually even if not immediately. Hostility to Liberal social measures had declined greatly since 1911–12 and could not be relied upon to secure working-class votes. The land campaign launched by Lloyd George in 1913 threatened the Conservative position in the shires, but the party could not agree upon any constructive answer to this either. In 1914 the Conservatives seemed to be on the defensive, uttering only harsh and negative cries which principally appealed to their own most partisan supporters. They were not likely to lose many seats but would probably have gained too few to climb the electoral mountain before them. From this sterility the Irish question would not necessarily have rescued them. The question of the '1915 election' becomes doubly hypothetical in view of the fact that it would have taken place after Home Rule had become law, with unpredictable consequences. Unionists were convinced that the shedding of Protestant blood at the hands of the government or a Dublin parliament would provoke a mainland electoral backlash. However, if – and in view of the province's later history this seems not unlikely – violence instead took the form of a 'loyalist' pogrom of Ulster Catholics, there could equally have been a backlash against the party which had egged on resistance (**181**). In any case, after nearly thirty years of dispute there can have been few uncommitted votes still remaining to be won on the Irish issue.

All of these uncertainties were removed by the outbreak of war. Unlike the Liberals, the advent and conduct of the war presented no problems of principle or policy for the Conservatives. They felt that it vindicated their pre-war attitudes on tariff reform and German competition, and on the naval race and the need for military service. The war also exposed in their view the indecision and ineffectiveness of the Liberals. Partly through the mainly Conservative national press and partly due to the lack of military success in the field, the public came to share these sentiments. Inevitably, the position of the Liberals weakened whilst the

Conservatives grew in confidence and assertiveness. However, this process of political attrition took some time and it was not until the end of 1916 – and even then in partnership with Lloyd George – that it had full effect.

During the crisis of July 1914 the Conservative leaders pressured the Liberal Cabinet behind the scenes, insisting that Britain must honour its moral obligation to France and intervene to preserve the balance of power in Europe (**120**). The Liberal government remained in office, and as a 'patriotic opposition' the Conservatives could not attack it without endangering national unity and giving aid and comfort to the enemy. The most acute example of this was the government's decision to honour promises to its Irish supporters by placing the Home Rule Bill on the statute book, although accompanied by a measure suspending its operation until after the war. This caused great anger amongst Unionists, but 'they were imprisoned by their patriotism' and could no longer use their greatest weapon, the threat of civil strife in Ulster (**128**). Protest had to be limited to an expression of their objections by Bonar Law and a symbolic walkout from the Commons chamber. This may have been dramatic, but it underlined the impotence of an opposition in wartime. Conservatives were 'increasingly torn between a desire to support the war effort without propping up the government and an urge to attack the misconduct of the war without offending the patriotism of the electorate' (**124**). They felt that they were being asked to shoulder responsibility for decisions over which they had no influence, taken by a Cabinet in whom they had no confidence. These frustrations led to the creation of the Unionist Business Committee in January 1915. Chaired by Long, it had a regular attendance of around 40 backbench MPs. and pressed for the more effective prosecution of the war, concentrating upon such issues as munitions production, enemy aliens, and tariff and trade matters. The UBC was 'only the first of many devices that articulated party opinion against governments that the party theoretically supported' (**6**). However, this and later 'ginger groups' were also warning signals to the Conservative leaders that they were out of touch with their followers; in early 1915 this had been particularly the case over Lloyd George's plan for state control of the liquor trade.

The Conservative leaders had recognised the sterility of their position in early 1915; they had considered the possibility of coalition, but Bonar Law, in particular, resisted that solution [**doc. 11**]. However, within a few months the pressure of circumstance forced a change of view. Military and naval reverses on the Western and Eastern Fronts and at the Dardanelles made it clear that victory would not be swift, and that the government lacked a grip on the situation. The exact timing of the crisis which followed in May 1915 was the product of two unrelated factors: an imminent public scandal over the failure adequately to supply the armies in France with shells, and the resignation of the naval chief, Lord Fisher, after disputes over strategy with his political master, Winston Churchill. It was clear that both these issues would provoke a Conservative onslaught which Bonar Law would be unable to restrain, and in his view he had no patriotic alternative but to accept Asquith's invitation to enter a reshaped ministry. The first coalition was a party manoeuvre by Asquith, intended to maintain his personal control and to preserve the dominance of the Liberals. Conservative ministers were excluded from the most significant posts – apart from Balfour, sent to the Admiralty in a partly successful attempt to diminish Law's standing as leader.

The impact of the Great War

Conservatives showed their patriotism and enthusiasm for the war in a number of ways. Of the party's local agents 125 served in the armed forces, whilst at any one time more than 100 Conservative MPs were absent from the House on military duties. The party organisation was involved from the outset in a joint recruiting drive with the Liberals, providing local offices, manpower and expertise. After the flood of volunteers began to ebb, the Conservative machine was employed in administering the 'Derby scheme' of November 1915 and other recruitment measures through to the adoption of full conscription, and many local associations were involved in 1917 in the War Savings and War Aims campaigns. With the need for increased controls and rationing in everyday life as the war developed, many Conservative agents took up posts in the new government departments. In most cases these were in their own locality, and they were able to keep the party machinery in being. Although local activity generally declined in 1917, the changes to constituency boundaries in the 1918 Reform Act stimulated a revival, either to contest the Commissioners' proposals or to establish associations for the new seats. At national level the National Union met regularly from 1917 onwards, even holding a special conference in late 1917.

As the war continued during 1915 many previous sources of conflict faded into the background. The new public priorities favoured the Conservatives as the party identified with patriotism, strong defences and the unfettered prosecution of the war. Even before 1914 many Conservatives had advocated conscription, and the party had little objection to enlarging the directing powers of the state in wartime. In this situation Conservatives were 'sure about ends and pragmatic as to means' (**6**). This was not the case with the Liberal Party, and the resulting tensions underlay the rift between Asquith and Lloyd George which developed in 1916. Throughout its life the Asquith coalition 'functioned not as a national coalition of equals but as a party coalition of unequal and often mutually suspicious rivals' (**127**). With these flaws, it proved to be neither a happy nor an effective regime. As the personal prestige and control of the premier declined steadily during 1916, the surprise is not that the Asquith coalition fell but rather that it lasted as long as it did. There were two issues in particular which produced protracted wrangling in the Cabinet. The first of these was compulsory military service, over which Asquith retreated step by step until it was finally introduced in full in May 1916; the second was Ireland, where in the aftermath of the Easter rising of 1916 Lloyd George attempted to negotiate a solution based upon the immediate application of Home Rule outside Ulster. This was accepted by most Conservative leaders on the grounds that it gave them their demands of 1914 and had been accepted by the Ulster Unionists. However, the plan foundered due to its own contradictions and to opposition on behalf of the southern Irish Unionists led by Long and Lansdowne (**128**).

These issues were also aspects of the greater problem of the higher direction of the war, the dilatoriness of Asquith, and the premier's reliance upon conventional peacetime methods of business. Unionists were frustrated by the failure of the government to grapple with decisions in sufficient time or to demonstrate that it had a grip on the war; they feared and anticipated an erosion of public confidence. From the autumn of 1915 backbenchers became distanced from their leaders and accustomed to voting against the Cabinet in which they seemed almost to have become prisoners. After Carson's resignation in October 1915, MPs had an alternative leader around whom to gather, and his power base became the Unionist War Committee, founded in January 1916. This was a larger and more significant body than the UBC, for its membership of around 150 included almost every

Unionist MP who was not either in the ministry or absent on service. However, it was similar in origin to the UBC, being a manifestation of backbench unease over the compromises made by the party leaders and unhappiness over the lack of progress and energy in the war effort. One of the few ministers to impress in 1915–16 was Lloyd George, but although his vigour and dexterity were recognised he was still distrusted by most Unionist leaders. For a long time Bonar Law could see no suitable alternative to Asquith; his continued loyalty ensured the ministry's survival but was to make his own position as leader vulnerable. The Nigeria debate of November 1916 provided the opportunity for a back-bench protest which forced Law to reassess the future of the Coalition (**127**). After this he took the crucial decision to work with Carson and Lloyd George in demanding the reconstruction of the machinery of government along more effective lines. The complex events of the resulting crisis of December 1916 have given rise to much controversy, but it is clear that the other Unionist ministers supported this aim, and when forced to choose they were willing to displace Asquith and serve under Lloyd George in order to achieve it (**129, 123**).

The recast Coalition which Lloyd George led between 1916 and 1918 was a genuine partnership based upon consensus about aims and methods. Conservative leaders now moved into positions of key authority: Law as Chancellor of the Exchequer and deputy Prime Minister formed one of the five-man war cabinet, along with Curzon and Milner, whilst the party also held the Foreign Office, Home Office, War Office, Admiralty and other key ministries. At the heart of the government lay the close and equal working relationship between Bonar Law and Lloyd George. The new administration's commitment to total war secured the loyalty of the Conservative Party in the Commons and the country and saw it through the strains and stresses of 1917–18, although Lloyd George's reappointment of Churchill to the Cabinet produced angry protests. In the strategic debate over the military stalemate between 1914 and 1918, most Conservatives were uncritical supporters of the general staff and thus were 'westerners' rather than 'easterners', giving highest priority to the demands of the Western Front. This led to tension with Lloyd George, who lacked confidence in the military commanders. Rather than go directly through a problem, Lloyd George always preferred to circle round it, even if as a result he ended up appearing to face the other way. Conservatives at all levels were always uneasily aware of this characteristic, but it only became a serious problem when it was linked with successive failures after 1920.

The Conservative Party emerged from the First World War with its prestige as a successful party of government restored by its vigorous presence in the Lloyd George Coalition Cabinet, and it shared with him the popular credit for victory. The Conservatives were the only party to have been clearly and unequivocally committed to the war effort all the way through, without internal division and disagreement. The experience of war had also validated the party's stand in several respects at the expense of its rivals. The most obvious of these were defence expenditure and conscription, but pure free trade had been abandoned by a Liberal Chancellor of the Exchequer with the McKenna duties of 1915, whilst the contribution made by the dominion forces underlined the value and importance of the empire. The events of 1914–18 had created a different political agenda in Britain; Ireland, the House of Lords and even tariff reform no longer seemed so central. The fundamental landmarks of the Edwardian era had been replaced by 'a host of new challenges that could not be dealt with successfully by pre-war solutions' (**127**). Attention was focused instead upon the role of the state in society and the economy, social reform, unemployment and the rise of Labour. During the war the trade unions had grown considerably in numbers and influence, and with them the potential strength of the Labour Party. One Conservative response to this was the promotion of alternative groups claiming to represent 'patriotic labour', in the hope that they would wean working-class support away from the 'pacifist' Labour Party. Amongst the leaders the strongest advocate of this strategy was Milner, but the scepticism of Central Office was proved correct, for none of these initiatives made any lasting impression.

With Bolshevism threatening to sweep across much of Europe in 1918–20, and with industrial unrest and the strains of demobilisation at home, there was considerable fear of instability and revolution. In such an atmosphere it was natural for the Conservatives, unsure of the political impact of the extended franchise, to favour the continuation of the wartime Coalition. It was not just the euphoria of long-awaited victory but also sober calculation which led Bonar Law and other Conservative leaders to this decision. Within the government Conservatives and Coalition Liberals had worked well together and become accustomed to the arrangement: faced with dangerous waters ahead there seemed no gain and great risks in dividing the forces of 'constitutionalism' in the face of the challenge of Socialism [**doc. 12**]. In 1918–20 national interest and party interest seemed to coincide in support for Coalition: 'in this case more than in most, the two types of motive blended and reinforced each other' (**117**). An agreed programme was worked out without difficulty, although some of the pledges in it on tariffs, reform of the House of Lords and Ireland led to problems later. The Conservative rank and file accepted continuation of the Coalition without dissent: not only did they defer to their leaders' united judgement in such matters, but they also shared the same concerns. In addition, an appeal for national unity was bound to strike a chord with most Conservatives (**122**).

The general election was held immediately after the armistice in December 1918, and was a landslide for the Coalition. Official candidates were identified to the electors by the receipt of a letter of endorsement signed by both Lloyd George and Bonar Law, dubbed the 'coupon' by Asquith. This was primarily a device to shelter Lloyd George's followers from a Conservative landslide, and about 150 'coupons' were issued to Liberal candidates. During the campaign there was some friction between Conservative Central Office and Lloyd George's whips and managers over precise allocations, but on the whole a complex and potentially fractious process was handled effectively. The strength of the Conservative Party was shown by the total number of candidates which it ran; its popular support was demonstrated by the success of many of those who stood without benefit of the 'coupon', one of whom defeated Asquith. The Conservatives accounted for 382 of the 523 Coalition MPs elected, whilst only 28 independent Liberals and 63 Labour MPs were returned. A new political landscape was revealed: the Liberal Party was fatally divided, the Conservatives had recovered vitality to become the dominant political force, and the Labour Party had weathered the storm to emerge as their principal challengers. Finally and perhaps most importantly, developments in Ireland removed the solid bloc of around 85 Irish Nationalist MPs who had consistently supported the Liberal Party since Gladstone's adoption of Home Rule in 1886. In the general election of 1918 the old Irish party of Parnell and Redmond was swept away by Sinn Fein, but the new MPs refused to take their seats at Westminster, and the seats themselves disappeared in 1922 as a result of the Anglo-Irish Treaty. After the partition, the only Irish MPs in the House of Commons came from the North, and almost all of these were Ulster Unionists who for all practical purposes counted as Conservative MPs. Ireland, so long a barrier to the Conservatives, now became an asset.

Not only the balance of parties but also the electoral system underwent a radical change. The Conservative Party was initially hostile to the proposals which emerged from the Speaker's conference in May 1917, but when legislation was introduced only 40 MPs were willing to vote against it. Anticipating a possible wartime election, Conservatives were keen to ensure that servicemen would get the vote, and the party was also favourable to some form of female suffrage. There was little point in contesting the principle, and as the proposals passed through Parliament in 1917 attention was concentrated instead upon the defence of specific details. The Conservatives succeeded in retaining the university seats and the business vote, both of which were overwhelmingly to their advantage. The party also benefited from the redistribution of seats which formed part of the Act eventually passed in 1918. Conservative seats in the Home Counties with expanding populations were sub-divided to form several new constituencies, whilst many Liberal seats with small electorates in the West, the North and in Scotland disappeared. The Reform Act of 1918 introduced a democratic electorate by giving the vote to men at the age of 21 and women at 30, with only minor exclusions. This extension of the franchise to male voters previously excluded is often supposed to have assisted the rise of Labour. However, the new male voters were not entirely working-class, and of those who were, some were susceptible to the Conservative appeal, especially in the atmosphere of 'Hang the Kaiser' in 1918. This was still more true of the women of all classes who were now enfranchised for the first time, and during the inter-war period the Conservative Party consistently secured the largest share of the female vote.

The First World War also affected the Conservative Party in three other ways. First, it stimulated the growth of backbench activity and assertiveness in the parliamentary party: the UBC and UWC were the foundation upon which the permanent structures of the 1922 Committee and the official 'subject' committees were later built in the mid-1920s (**52**). Second, the extensions of the franchise in 1918 to men and women of all classes meant that substantial reshaping and expansion of the party organisation at national and local level would be required to respond to this. Third, the experience of the trenches brought many young officers from public school and university into close contact with the working class for the first time. This had a lasting impact upon the views of many of the younger MPs who entered Parliament in the 1920s, such as Harold Macmillan and Anthony Eden.

The fall of the Coalition

The basis for Conservative revival and success in the inter-war period lay in the changes wrought by the Great War and the choices which the party made between 1918 and 1924. The most crucial of these was whether Conservatives should stand alone and face the new democracy with confidence or merge their identity with others in a broad-based 'constitutional' alliance. Three principal themes were articulated by the Conservative supporters of Coalition after 1918. First was the fear of a Socialist government gaining power and perhaps opening the way to more extreme revolutionaries, as the Kerensky regime had in Russia. Second was the difficulty of ensuring stable and effective government in abnormal times. Finally, related to this, were economic and external problems too intractable for one party alone to cope with (**117**). The post-war Coalition had thus both a negative and a positive appeal. It offered the security of a defensive anti-Socialist front, but this contained seeds of danger, for inevitably it promoted an atmosphere of class warfare, of capital versus labour. When the immediate fears of social and industrial breakdown receded after 1921, to be replaced by the less threatening challenge of a Labour Party committed to orthodox parliamentary politics, many Conservatives came to regard this aspect of the Coalition as provocative and divisive. Evidence that it might actually be counter-productive was provided by the success of Labour candidates, and the dismal failure of Coalition Liberals, in by-elections from 1920 onwards (**118**).

The Coalition's positive appeal was developed through ambitious schemes of reconstruction, mainly the work of progressive Liberal ministers such as Addison and Fisher (**122**). In the atmosphere of victory, unity and 'homes for heroes', Conservatives at all levels were genuinely willing to support bold plans, especially if they would provide social stability. Problems emerged therefore not in 1918–19 but after 1920, when the post-war boom collapsed and recession made the Conservative rank and file pressingly aware of the cost of these measures. Taxation and inflation both stood at record levels in 1920, whilst the continuation of many of the new wartime departments made the government seem extravagant and bureaucratic. Conservative leaders in the Cabinet were slow to respond to their supporters' demands for 'economy' and so left the door open for the press baron Lord Rothermere. He promoted the 'Anti-Waste League' which articulated the growing grass-roots alienation from the Coalition and from their leaders. The League began to score by-election successes, and the response of the Cabinet bore all the hallmarks of panic. Schemes of social reform were abandoned, Addison was forced into resignation, and the Geddes Committee was established with a brief to slash government expenditure. Ironically, an early victim of retrenchment was the Agriculture Act of 1920; although costly, this was regarded as vital by the farmers, and many rural Conservative MPs felt betrayed by its sudden repeal (**57**).

The proposal to make the Coalition permanent by merging the parties which supported it into a single 'Centre Party' was dropped in 1920, because of the antipathy of the Liberal ministers, but there had been little Conservative enthusiasm for 'fusion' either. From this point onwards the component parts drifted slowly apart, with mounting friction and Conservative restiveness in the constituencies. Another symptom of decay was the emergence of the 'diehards' in 1921, a coherent group of 40–50 Conservative backbenchers who were openly hostile to the Coalition and denounced its betrayal of 'Unionist principles'. In fact, the Coalition was undermined by its own failures rather than the attacks of its enemies, most of whom were discredited, ineffective or obscure, talking only to themselves (**122**). The government provided its critics with plentiful ammunition in almost every area of policy, not least because of too many sudden and unpredictable reversals of direction. Most painful to Unionists was the abandonment of southern Ireland to the rebels in the negotiations and treaty of 1921. This settlement did, however, guarantee the independence of Ulster, and was endorsed by the annual conference in November 1921 as the only practical way out of the morass; but steadying the nerves of the party required the united authority of the hierarchy and used up much of their credit. Other issues which cumulatively increased Conservative disaffection were the Liberal policy of Montagu on India, symbolised by the censure of General Dyer after the Amritsar massacre, and the making of diplomatic overtures to Bolshevik Russia. In domestic policy the recession brought friction over demands for 'safeguarding', a form of limited industrial protection, and over legislative action on two issues of great concern to a Conservative rank and file fearful of the advance of Labour – the 'reform' of the House of Lords and the compulsory trade-union political levy (**121**). After these fiascos or disappointments, the only arguments still remaining in favour of coalition by the summer of 1922 were the purely negative ones.

As the party's mood began to change, its sense of security was further shaken by the sudden retirement of Bonar Law for reasons of health in March 1921. His continued presence at the centre of affairs had reassured many who had come to regard other leading Coalitionists – in particular, F.E. Smith and Winston Churchill – as opportunistic and unprincipled adventurers whose only interest was in their own advancement. Long had also retired in the month before; as no other contenders had emerged, the leadership passed to Austen Chamberlain without debate. However, he had little time to settle into the post and his limitations soon became apparent: he lacked imagination, remained aloof from his subordinates and was too inflexible. Although Chamberlain was personally trusted and respected, he did not appear to stand up to Lloyd George as Law had done, and this unbalanced the vital relationship which preserved the party's tolerance of the Coalition. Bound by his sense of honour and loyalty to support the continuation of the Coalition, Chamberlain was unable and unwilling to assert its Conservative identity and reassure those who feared that the party was losing its independence (**30**, **46**). The crucial issue was not whether to continue in an anti-Socialist alliance with the National Liberals, but in what manner and under whose leadership. There were two alternatives. The first was to enter the coming election in an informal partnership and then to reconstruct the government afterwards, according to the resulting balance of forces. This strategy would ensure a Conservative Prime Minister and a more Conservative tone of policy, and it implied the subordination of Lloyd George (**118**). It was therefore the choice favoured by the constituency activists and backbench MPs outside the most marginal districts, and by the party managers, whips and most of the junior ministers. It clearly had overwhelming support in the National Union, whose annual conference scheduled for November 1922 was certain to make embarrassing demands for separation. However, Austen Chamberlain and the most powerful Conservative Cabinet ministers dismissed this sentiment with a haughty contempt towards factious partisans akin to that of Peel – and they suffered the same fate. They saw no alternative to fighting the election with Lloyd George as Prime Minister; if the Coalition, as they assumed, was triumphant once again, there could be no question of expecting the Premier to step aside in his hour of victory. They therefore attempted to suppress the pressures rising from below (most notoriously in the counter-productive harangue which Chamberlain permitted Birkenhead to deliver to an anxious but still loyal group of junior ministers on 3 August 1922), and they sought to manoeuvre the party into an election and to by-pass the National Union (**179, 182**).

The first such attempt in January 1922 was thwarted from an unexpected direction when the Party Chairman, Sir George Younger, circularised the constituencies condemning the idea of an early election and pointing to the unfulfilled pledges, especially on House of Lords reform. This led to public fulminations from leading Coalitionists that the 'cabin boy' had grasped the helm, and their onslaught upon Younger in its turn provoked the National Union to rally round him [**doc. 13**]. From then onwards the intentions of the leaders were regarded with suspicion by a much wider circle in the party than just the 'diehards', with both Central Office and the whips drifting into the hostile camp. Despite the warnings relayed by his party managers, Austen Chamberlain failed to see the deficiencies in the Coalition or its approaching danger. He trusted too much in the dwindling capital of the leadership's authority, and made the mistake of considering the present Cabinet elite irreplaceable. In fact the failures of policy both at home and abroad had discredited ministers and made many long to sweep them from office. Despite the 1921 treaty there was renewed strife in Ireland, whilst in June 1922 the recently elected Ulster MP and wartime commander, Sir Henry Wilson, was assassinated on his London doorstep. Despite the efforts of the Geddes Committee to apply the axe, expenditure and taxation remained high and the economy stagnated. A major scandal over the sale of peerages was sparked by the appearance of several particularly unsuitable names in the honours list in July. Matters such as this affronted Conservative sentiment and seemed to confirm the 'whiff of corruption' which in their eyes had attached to Lloyd George since the Marconi affair of 1913. In foreign affairs the much-heralded Genoa conference in April 1922 was a fiasco. Reckless support of Greek ambitions in Asia Minor led after their collapse to a confrontation with revived Turkish nationalism in the Chanak crisis of September: in the course of this the Cabinet seemed bent upon provoking war whilst simultaneously alienating the dominions (**122**). This was the last straw. Bonar Law fired a warning shot in a letter to *The Times* declaring that 'Britain alone could not be the policeman of the world', and considered emerging from his retirement.

It was against this dismal background that Austen Chamberlain, fearing further deterioration in the position over the approaching winter, decided to force a confrontation. He summoned a party meeting of MPs to the Carlton Club for 19 October 1922, a month before the annual conference was due to gather. By doing so he forced others to take sides: reluctantly, most chose to differ from Chamberlain's analysis of the situation and to reject his solution [**doc. 14**]. Under severe pressure from their constituency Executives, many MPs had already promised to run as 'independent Conservatives' at the next election (**121**). In the final few days before the meeting the junior ministers rallied the dissenters, helped by leading moderate backbenchers such as Sir Samuel Hoare. They were openly supported by two Cabinet ministers, Stanley Baldwin and Arthur Griffith-Boscawen, who indicated their intention to resign (**118**). Although they were amongst the least prominent in the Cabinet, Baldwin in particular was trusted by and in close touch with the majority feeling of the middle and lower ranks of the party. The Coalitionists were also shaken by the more private, eleventh-hour defection of the Foreign Secretary, Lord Curzon. On the morning of the meeting, the case for the Coalition was further undermined by the result of the Newport by-election held on the previous day, where an 'independent Conservative' was challenging both the Coalition Liberal and Labour in an industrial seat. Chamberlain expected this split would let Labour win, and deliberately timed the Carlton Club meeting so that the danger of a rift would be clear; when the Conservative came top of the poll and the Coalitionist trailed at the bottom, the opposite lesson was drawn (**125**).

At the meeting itself Chamberlain opened with a lengthy exposition and was supported by a call for loyalty from Balfour, but it was clear that both were out of touch with the mood of their audience. Baldwin briefly but effectively warned that Lloyd George would divide the Conservatives as badly as he already had the Liberals. However, the crucial factor was Bonar Law's decision to attend and thereby put himself at the head of the revolt and provide it with a credible popular alternative as leader and Prime Minister. The ballot gave a decisive margin in favour of independence, by 185 to 88, and immediately afterwards Lloyd George resigned as Premier and Austen Chamberlain as leader, with Bonar Law taking the place of both. The minority who voted with Chamberlain at the

Carlton Club contained many MPs who had first entered the Commons in 1918 for industrial seats in the Midlands, the North and Scotland, where success had depended upon securing former Liberal votes. The majority included most of those sitting for safe and traditionally Conservative constituencies in the South, and the 'diehards', in particular, contained more MPs who had sat before 1918 and more who came from gentry and military backgrounds. The split was one of North versus South, marginal versus safe, and of left versus right in terms of political outlook.

6 The Age of Baldwin, 1922–39

The recovery of unity

The fall of the Lloyd George Coalition was the most serious internal revolt in the history of the Conservative Party during the twentieth century, for it led to the dismissal of the Prime Minister, the Conservative leader and almost all of the party's senior front-benchers. The crucial questions of the next two years were the competence of those who replaced them, the terms of any reunion and the fear of a revived Coalition. The restoration of Conservative unity took time, for the scars of rejection ran deep and the leading Coalitionists continually overestimated their own importance and underrated the abilities of their opponents. They saw themselves as a more experienced and competent alternative leadership, and were dismissive of their successors as 'second-class brains' and a government of 'the second eleven'. For this reason they remained aloof and asked too high a price, demanding to be negotiated with as a group. This the new leadership never needed or was willing to do, although periodic offers were made on an individual basis (**118**). In fact, time was not on the Coalitionists' side, for in the parliamentary party their support steadily dwindled and at constituency level it was non-existent. The Conservative split in 1922 was a horizontal slice across the top and not a vertical one evenly dividing the party at every level, and this was one reason why it did not lead to long-term damage similar to that suffered by the Liberals after 1916. There was no doubt where the bulk of Conservative opinion lay, and by a natural force of political gravity this slowly drew the Coalitionists back into the party mainstream. Equally crucial in containing the damage was the restraint gener-ally shown by Law and Baldwin on the one side and Austen Chamberlain on the other: whatever their private feelings, a public feud was avoided. Only Birkenhead did not conform to the party's instinct for solidarity, and his reward was the deep antagonism of most MPs (**22**). Above all, disunity was not carried into the con-stituencies. There was no purge of MPs and almost no competing candidatures, and the fragmentation of the local organisation and of the Conservative vote was avoided.

Immediately after forming his government, Bonar Law dissolved Parliament, and a general election was held in November 1922. The Conservatives fought this as a separate party: there were local deals with Coalition Liberals in many areas which were tacitly encouraged by Central Office, but there was no formal alliance. Three hundred and forty-four Conservative MPs were returned: against most expectations the party had secured a governing majority in its own right for the first time since 1900, and the Law government continued in office (**121**). The Lloyd George Liberals lost seats to both the Conservatives and Labour, which became the official opposition for the first time. The Labour advance polarised politics to the benefit of the Conservatives and the detriment of the Liberals, collapsing the centre ground from beneath the latter's feet. Bonar Law had campaigned in 1922 on a deliberately vague and negative platform, avoiding controversial commitments and appealing to the demand for consistency and a return to normality summed up in the slogan 'tranquillity'. This may have been sound tactics in an election which was almost a referendum on the Lloyd George regime, but it did not provide an effective basis for government. In the early months of 1923 the ministry was visibly drifting. This was due to Law's belief that a period of calm would restore business confidence and the economy, to his style of leadership and to his declining health. The government nearly fell apart in January 1923, when Law had to be persuaded not to resign over his hostility to the terms negotiated by Baldwin for the repayment of war debt to the United States (**20**). These developments only served to confirm the Coalitionists' belief that the Cabinet would collapse, due to its inexperience and inadequacy, and so Austen Chamberlain declined an invitation from Law to rejoin in April 1923. As a result, when Law's health finally and suddenly failed a few weeks later, Chamberlain was still in exile and so could not be considered as his replacement.

The choice of leader in May 1923 lay between the two principal figures in the ministry. Lord Curzon, Foreign Secretary since 1919, was by far the more experienced contender. His rival, Stanley Baldwin, had only entered the Cabinet in 1921 and became Chancellor of the Exchequer after the fall of the Coalition largely by default. The issue was not one of policy – for both were anti-Coalitionists – but of personality. It was complicated by Law's doubts about both men, which led to his refusal to recommend a successor to the King, who had to take soundings of his own and effectively select the new leader. The matter of how this was decided and who influenced the monarch has caused much debate (**20, 143, 176**). In fact the choice was simple, for Baldwin had three crucial advantages. First, he would be more able to reunite the party as his open dissent in 1922 was much less resented by the Coalitionists than Curzon's last-minute 'ratting' to the winning side. Second, the latter's pompous and arrogant manner had alienated his Cabinet colleagues: it was known that the key figure of Lord Derby would serve under Baldwin but not under Curzon. Finally, and perhaps of greatest weight with the King, the selection of Curzon as Prime Minister in the House of Lords would be socially divisive and provocative because the Labour Party was almost unrepresented in the upper chamber. Curzon did not foresee this and was shocked and humiliated when he was passed over, but the choice of Baldwin was a turning point in the party's fortunes and a key factor in its success during the next fifteen years.

At first this was far from apparent, for within a few months Baldwin had led the party into an unnecessary defeat, throwing away a majority which could have run for a full parliament in a reckless and botched appeal for a mandate for tariffs. The factors which led to the general election of December 1923 are neither as subtle or convoluted as Baldwin himself and later historians have suggested (**150**). The idea that Baldwin intended to lose an election, even in order to achieve the reunion of the party on his own terms, is patently absurd. Defeat would be divisive and dangerous, and would probably abruptly terminate his leadership. The truth is much simpler, and stemmed from the problems of policy which the government was facing by the autumn of 1923. The change of Prime Minister had not altered the fact that the ministry appeared to be dull and drifting, without imagination or distinctive policies. The Labour Party was mounting an emotive campaign on the unemployment issue as the country approached a fourth successive winter of economic stagnation, but efforts to revive trade by securing stability in Europe had been thwarted due to friction with France. A bold initiative to recover authority and enthuse the party was needed, and economic and political pressures naturally turned Conservative thoughts towards tariff reform. This was being urged by the 'diehards', who had been left outside the Cabinet and might again become a divisive force; more importantly, by August moderate Cabinet ministers were leaning in the direction of protection. Tariffs could not be limited to manufacturing industry alone: the agricultural depression raised the issue of food taxes for domestic rather than imperial purposes. The final impetus was given by the dominion premiers' renewed call for preferential links at the Imperial Conference of October 1923. Rumours that Lloyd George would seize upon protection as the basis of a Coalitionist coup were given credence by Central Office, but although this may have influenced the timing of the announcement it was not its cause (**150**).

The government were still bound by the pledge not to introduce tariffs which Law had given during the 1922 campaign, and so Baldwin's decision to opt for protection inevitably required an appeal to the country. The Prime Minister presented his plan to the Cabinet on 23 October, and began preparing the ground for a spring election with his speech to the party conference at Plymouth two days later. This naïve strategy swiftly proved untenable, for the speech created great uncertainty and effectively launched an undeclared election campaign. The situation slipped out of control, and by 9 November the Cabinet had accepted the need for an immediate election, with polling fixed for the earliest possible date of 6 December. The possibility of Conservative reunion was a secondary consideration and only taken up by Baldwin at this point. After some confusion, he was able both to deter the free-trade Cabinet ministers from resigning and to secure on his own terms the active support of Austen Chamberlain and Birkenhead (**118**). However, if the leadership entered the 1923 election remarkably united, the lower ranks of the party did not. Neither the policy nor the organisation proved able to cope with the stress of the campaign, and the negative cry of 'stomach taxes' once again proved too much. Despite 20 gains there was a net Conservative loss of 88 seats, and the result created a difficult parliamentary situation. With 258 MPs the Conservatives were still the largest party in the House of Commons, but their majority had gone and they had clearly lost the election (**140**). Of the two free-trade parties, Labour had 191 MPs to the Liberals' 158, and a first minority Labour government was the most likely outcome when Parliament met in January 1924. The events of 1923 might seem to have proven the Coalitionist case; in fact they effectively killed it. Despite some initial Conservative panic, it became clear that the bulk of the party did not regret the decision of 1922 and would rather risk a Labour ministry tamed by its minority status than return to the embrace of Lloyd George [**docs 15, 16**]. The intrigues which bred in the febrile weeks of December 1923 all foundered upon the twin rocks of this sentiment and the lack of any acceptable alternative to Baldwin (**26**). Once he decided not to resign but to meet Parliament and force the Liberals to vote Labour into office, the party had no alternative but to support him. Anger and tension over the defeat took some time to dissipate, but Baldwin's personal standing in the country had risen and his leadership was endorsed without opposition at a party meeting on 11 February 1924.

By this time three important events had taken place: the Coalition rift had been healed, the tariff policy had been dropped, and Labour had come into office. Baldwin was determined that Labour should not be denied their chance, which he saw would strengthen the moderates and give the leaders a taste of responsibility. Conservative unity was achieved by the incorporation of the former Coalitionists into the shadow cabinet at its first meeting on 7 February 1924, a natural progression after the support which they had given during the election campaign. At the same meeting it was also decided to shelve the full tariff programme and revert to the much less controversial policy of 'safeguarding'. Established by an Act of 1921, this permitted industries which could demonstrate that they were facing unfair or subsidised foreign competition to make a formal application for limited and targeted protection. Safeguarding was to be the foundation of Conservative policy until 1930; it could be popular, as it helped only those industries threatened with decline and consequent unemployment. It could not be applied to agriculture, nor, implicitly, could it be extended to the largest sectors of the manufacturing economy, as that would effectively introduce a general tariff by the back door. The events of February 1924 healed the wounds left by the split of 1922 and cleared the air after the defeat of 1923. It was clear that the inexperienced minority Labour government would not last many months, and the Conservatives turned in a positive rather than negative spirit to an ambitious reappraisal of policy and organisation. Baldwin began a campaign of speeches of studied moderation and high morality which enhanced his appeal to the general public. MPs were occupied by a series of policy committees, each covering an area of government and chaired by the relevant ex-minister; the results of their deliberations were published on 20 June under the title *Looking Ahead*. After the party returned to power later in 1924, these 'subject' committees continued to function under elected backbench chairmen, and ever since, in parallel with the more general forum of the 1922 Committee, they have been the basis of the party's parliamentary organisation.

In the House of Commons, disciplined tactics thwarted much of Labour's efforts and frequently led to Liberal fragmentation; ultimately, on 8 October 1924, the Liberals were manoeuvred into combining with the Conservatives to eject the government over the Campbell case, and the third general election within two years ensued. This time the Conservatives were strongly placed: they were united and resolute, their organisation had revived, they had ditched their unpopular tariff policy in favour of moderate and attractive proposals on housing, pensions and welfare, and they could plausibly offer stability in government. The party had easy targets to attack: the Liberals for putting Labour in, and Labour for their alarming rhetoric. The Campbell affair, in which the government appeared to have stopped the prosecution of the Communist editor of the *Daily Worker*, and Labour's proposed treaty with Russia were material enough: the appearance of the 'Zinoviev letter' in the final days of the campaign may have given further impetus but was not in itself a decisive factor. The Conservatives managed to get the best of both worlds: whilst most candidates and many ministers indulged in the 'Red scare' to the full, Baldwin remained above the fray on a higher plane of studied reason and moderation (**140**). This maximised the party's appeal to former Liberal voters, many of whom now had no candidate of their own to vote for. As a result the Conservatives gained 154 seats and with 412 MPs secured the biggest total ever achieved by a party fighting on its own merits and without allies; truly 1924 is the forgotten landslide of British electoral history.

Electoral success between the wars

The electoral record of the Conservative Party between the wars was one of remarkable success. They won landslide victories in 1918, 1924 and 1931, and only between 1929 and 1931 were they not the largest single party in the House of Commons. Alone or as the principal partner in a coalition the Conservatives held office for over 25 of the 29 years from 1916 to 1945. Whilst events, issues, policies and leaders all played their part in this, the basis of the improvement in the party's fortunes was the impact of the First World War and the changes to the electoral and party system which followed in 1918–21. Taken together, these had 'transformed the Unionists from the natural minority they had been in 1914 to a natural majority party' (**6**). There were a larger number of safe Conservative seats with a significant suburban and middle-class element than ever before. These produced a bedrock of 200 constituencies which consistently returned Conservatives, together with a further 100–140 which in varying degrees were frequently winnable. With the House of Commons reduced to 615 MPs after 1921, only 308 seats were now required for a bare majority. Despite the fact that most of the contests between the wars were three-party battles, the Conservative Party's share of the total national vote never fell below 38 per cent.

The general elections of 1918 and 1922 exposed the split within the Liberal Party and hastened its decline. The Conservative Party secured the adherence of few former Liberal ministers or MPs in comparison with the much larger drift to the Labour Party; the most prominent Liberal to join the Conservatives, Winston Churchill, appeared for many years to be more of a liability than an asset. However, this obscures the fact that at the lower level of Liberal supporters and voters the benefits were much more evenly shared between the Conservative and Labour parties. The Liberal decline is too often discussed solely in relation to the rise of the Labour Party. Labour certainly gained former Liberal seats in the larger urban and industrial areas, but in the suburbs, the small towns and especially in the rural areas it was the Conservatives who succeeded to the Liberal inheritance. In this they were often assisted by the appearance of Labour candidates who had little chance of winning such seats, but who drew away a portion of the Liberal supporters. The struggle between the Liberal and Labour parties for the left-of-centre in British politics thus appeared greatly to benefit the Conservatives, who were able to win the general election of 1922 with only 38.5 per cent of the poll (**121**). However, the latter figure does not allow for the 42 Conservatives returned unopposed or the fact that, despite the repudiation of formal coalition at Cabinet level, there were still many informal local pacts with the Lloyd George Liberals in 1922, especially in the North and in Scotland.

In fact, the division on the left of British politics was not a guarantee of success for the right: of the four general elections held during the 1920s, the Conservatives won two and lost two. The two defeats, in 1923 and 1929, occurred when the issues or the public mood did not favour the Conservatives and when they faced a confident Labour Party and a fairly united and effective Liberal Party. On the two occasions when the Conservatives won, the Liberal Party was either still badly divided (in 1922) or, through internal wrangling, unwilling and financially unable to run a large number of candidates (in 1924). The best scenario for the Conservative Party was a Liberal absence from the poll and a large number of straight fights against Labour, of which there were 111 in 1922, a drop to 100 in 1923, and a steep rise to 207 in 1924. Thus a crucial difference between the massive victory for the Conservatives in 1924 and their defeat at the next election in 1929 lay in the Liberal revival promoted by Lloyd George and the response of Liberal voters. In 1924 many Liberals were influenced by fear of Socialism, and with only 339 Liberal candidates standing, in many districts the Conservatives picked up vital Liberal support. Ironically, the Baldwin government's defeat of the General Strike in 1926 meant that by the time of the next general election in 1929 middle-class fear of Labour had considerably abated. With the Liberals now united under the energetic leadership of Lloyd George, with the propaganda value of his bold plans of public works to reduce unemployment, and with the help of his personal fund, 513 candidates were put up. Many Liberal voters returned to their old allegiance, and nearly all the Conservative gains of 1924 were lost. On the other hand, in the 1931 general election the Conservatives were the principal beneficiaries of the issues upon which the election was fought and of the mutual withdrawals which gave most Conservative candidates a straight fight against a Labour Party which had lost its leader and was in disarray (**153**). By the time of the following election in 1935 these two advantages had been diminished but not destroyed. The National Government's record in both domestic and foreign affairs was not uncreditable, and the coalition still contained half of the Liberal Party (the National Liberals led by Sir John Simon). Although the other half (led by Sir Herbert Samuel) had left the government over the issue of free trade in 1932 and was now in opposition, it was unable to field more than 161 candidates. Some marginal seats were gained by Labour as a result of this, but too few to make much impression upon the National Government's majority: when the results were in, the National Government had 429 MPs (of whom 387 were Conservatives), Labour 154 and the 'Samuelite' Liberals only 21.

It is impossible to make sense of the electoral statistics without acknowledging that a substantial portion – at least one-third – of the various social groups that are lumped together under the shorthand term of 'working-class' were intermittent or habitual Conservative supporters (**5, 134**). Not once between 1918 and 1935 was the Conservative total vote smaller than that of the Labour Party. The latter came closest in 1929, with 8.38 million votes to the Conservatives' 8.65 million; on this occasion the vagaries of the system gave Labour 288 MPs to only 260 for the Conservatives. In all the other general elections between the wars, Labour trailed the Conservatives in votes by between 1 and 5 million, and it was not until 1945 that the Labour Party secured a larger popular poll. The causes of working-class Conservatism are as many and varied as those which shape the political outlook of any other group, and it is a grave mistake to dismiss this particular manifestation of popular feeling as having been in some way misguided, mistaken or merely negative. There were sufficient positive factors to make the Conservative Party a repository of working-class votes: these ranged from the individual combinations of age, relative status, occupation, regional traditions, family influence and personal temperament, to the broad appeal of the party to national unity, patriotism, pride in the empire, independence, self-reliance and the search for prosperity at home without social upheaval and for peace abroad without military adventure (**134**). It was not necessary to have a large stake in the world to fear the advent of social chaos or revolution. These themes ran through the Conservative Party's posters and leaflets and the imagery and rhetoric of its politicians.

The organisational superiority of the Conservative Party between the wars was another factor in its electoral success. The Conservatives were more truly a national party than either the Liberals or Labour, with an active presence in every part of the country and in all types of constituency. The Conservative Party was financially stronger than its competitors at every level, and this underpinned both the large number of candidates which the party fielded in every election and the substantial network of full-time professional agents. For social and political reasons many local associations were able to attract a large membership, especially in the women's branches, and their regular programmes of events gave them a high profile in their own districts. Conservatism appeared in many places to be part of the natural fabric of society and almost non-political. At the national level the Conservatives were able to run a large and elaborate party machine, which was often the innovator in propaganda and campaigning methods (**6, 7, 61**). The party responded to the enfranchisements of 1918 by developing special organisations intended to recruit the new voters. The new women's wing was conspicuously successful, but another aimed at trade unionists was much less so, despite considerable Central Office effort and expenditure (**7**). The Conservative message was also reinforced by the preponderant support which it received from the press between the wars. This was the case at every level as Liberal newspapers merged and declined, leaving the field locally and nationally almost exclusively to the Conservative press. *The Times* and most other quality titles were steadfastly loyal to the party, as were many influential provincial newspapers. Although the leadership's relations with the mass-circulation popular press owned by Lords Beaverbrook and Rothermere were more uneven, with varying degrees of enthusiasm both of them backed the party at every general election. Against this avalanche of hostile comment the Labour Party only had the support of the *Daily Herald*, which was owned by the TUC.

Baldwin and the 'New Conservatism'

The personality of Stanley Baldwin, leader of the party from 1923 to 1937, also played an important part in Conservative electoral success. Baldwin came to prominence in the overthrow of the Lloyd George Coalition, and for many he symbolised the victory of honesty and principle over the cynical opportunism which they associated with Lloyd George and his circle. Even more significant was Baldwin's image of moderation. Despite deep Conservative anxiety over industrial unrest between the end of the war and the General Strike, Baldwin established his authority and political style by persuading the parliamentary party in 1925 not to support a 'diehard' MP's anti-trade-union Bill [**doc. 17**]. Baldwin's appeal for industrial harmony and peace between classes created a lasting impression upon both his audience in the House of Commons and the nation at large. He captured the spirit of the age: the widespread desire for tranquillity at home, peace and disarmament abroad, and a return wherever possible to pre-war verities (**45, 36**). He also made effective use of the two new forms of mass communication, the radio broadcast and the cinema newsreel (**67**). Although from a Worcestershire industrial family, he fostered the image of a traditional countryman who was as concerned for the welfare of the people as any rural squire would be for his villagers (**84**). Baldwin enjoyed widespread popularity with uncommitted Liberal and even Labour voters; his simple Christian ethic exerted a strong pull on the diffuse but still significant 'Nonconformist conscience'. Despite being defeated in 1929 on his own chosen strategy of 'Safety First', he was recognised to be the party's greatest electoral asset (**132**). Baldwin's style had its drawbacks, and it was only achieved at the cost of frequently thwarting the desires of the Conservative grass roots: this led to the apathy which partly caused the defeat of 1929, and to the crises over economic policy in 1929–31 and India in 1933–35. On the other hand, the National Government would probably not have been possible under any other Conservative leader. Baldwin's willingness to sit back and leave formal power to Ramsay MacDonald may have been the result of laziness and lack of ambition, but without it the National Government would hardly have lasted for more than a few months. With the Conservative Party electorally successful, and with a such a reassuring figure as Baldwin as its leader, the middle classes felt safe and secure. For this reason fascism failed to make any impact in Britain during the 1930s: the Conservative Party left no room for manoeuvre on the right, despite the moderation of its leadership (**139**). Even the most rebellious Conservatives preferred to remain and fight within the party, regarding the alternatives to it with derision.

Baldwin's 'New Conservatism' emerged between 1924 and 1926 and was encapsulated in three key statements: his speech to the party meeting of 11 February 1924, the pamphlet *Looking Ahead* of June 1924, and his oratorical triumph in the Macquisten debate of 6 March 1925 [**doc. 17**] – republished in the booklet *Peace in Industry*, this sold half a million copies in a few months. The images and assumptions underlying Baldwin's approach were further explored in the first collection of his speeches, *On England*, published in April 1926; his prestige and political style reached their zenith after the peaceful defeat of the General Strike in the following month. The 'New Conservatism' evoked the Disraelian 'One Nation' reformist tradition rather than the negativism of Salisbury or Law, and emphasised social harmony, industrial partnership, trust and confidence in the people, national interests and values, consensus and not confrontation. It was at the same time principled, distinctive, accessible, moderate and unprovocative; it involved social policies, generous by the standards of most governments, which were carried into effect by the Baldwin ministry of 1924–29 (**6**). 'Appeasement' had not yet become a dirty word and was an accurate motto for the Baldwinite approach both at home and abroad. It was understood to mean a sober but generous spirit of justice and conciliation proffered from a position of moral and physical strength; only after the foreign-policy failures of the 1930s was it redefined as a series of missed opportunities and concessions caused by weakness, irresolution and fear. In external affairs Conservative statesmen in the 1920s sought the return of stability in Europe in order to restore trade and thereby address a root cause of the stubbornly high level of domestic unemployment, termed the 'intractable million' by contemporary economists. Responsiveness to the popular post-war mood and to the accepted analysis of the causes of the Great War was combined with the recognition that Britain's strength was overstretched and its budget overburdened. Despite misgivings on the right which increased as the world situation deteriorated after 1929, this led to Conservative support for diplomacy through the League of Nations, negotiated disarmament, the abrogation of reparations, and a moderate imperial policy which entailed concessions to the demands of Egypt, India and the dominions.

In many ways Baldwin's second ministry of 1924–29 stands out as an oasis of normality in the troubled inter-war era. A single-party administration which lasted for nearly the full life of a parliament, its final years were free from domestic or international crises. There was an unusual degree of stability within the government and most Cabinet ministers served in the same post throughout. Even so, there was uncertainty at the beginning of its term. Fears of a Coalitionist plot were aroused in early 1925 by the 'cruiser crisis', a Cabinet dispute over naval expenditure between Bridgeman at the Admiralty and an economising Winston Churchill, the 'prodigal son' whom Baldwin had appointed Chancellor of the Exchequer to universal surprise and some hostility (**32**). The decision in July 1925 to purchase a breathing space in the strife-ridden coal industry with an interim subsidy was seen by many as a loss of nerve, especially following the refusal to legislate on the trade-union political levy. However, Baldwin and other senior ministers were convinced that, far from being a mandate for reaction, the victory of 1924 had been based upon the expectation of a programme of sensible reform which the party would fail to deliver at its peril. The government's major achievements all came within the first two years, and included in 1925 the Locarno agreements (negotiated by Austen Chamberlain who had returned as Foreign Secretary) and the provision of pensions for widows and orphans. The government's finest hour was the collapse of the General Strike in May 1926, after Baldwin, in a crucial radio broadcast, had portrayed it as an attack upon constitutional democracy.

From 1927 onwards there was a slow but steady decline, marked by ministerial illness and exhaustion. Cliques developed in the parliamentary ranks; the 'diehard' right became restive but were partly balanced by the smaller and more youthful 'YMCA' group on the left, who favoured corporatist intervention. The government was unable to mediate in the long coal strike of 1926–27, for despite having little liking for the owners it was impossible on ideological grounds to coerce them. Baldwin's hand seemed to have been forced by Cabinet hard-liners in the framing of the Trade Disputes Act of 1927. The raid on the Soviet trade delegation offices, Arcos, and the ensuing rupture of relations was one of many imprudent actions on the part of the Home Secretary, Sir William Joynson-Hicks. In foreign affairs the hopes built upon Locarno were not fulfilled, and disputes over naval disarmament caused serious friction with the United States. As Minister of Health, Neville Chamberlain was responsible for an impressive legislative programme, but his measures for factory, poor law and local government reform upset groups of Conservative supporters (**29**). Agriculture slid yet further into depression during the late 1920s, and in many rural areas the party's traditional bedrock felt neglected and alienated (**57**). Time and energy were unexpectedly consumed by the emotive issue of the new Prayer Book. The 'flapper vote' of 1928, equalising the franchise for both sexes at the age of 21, was disliked by the constituencies and later widely blamed for the 1929 defeat. Interventionist measures, moderate social policy and a failure to cut expenditure disappointed many supporters. By 1929 a rising chorus of complaint that the Prime Minister and his policies were 'semi-Socialist' could be heard from disaffected businessmen in the provinces and in the City. There was growing resentment of the failure to use the huge majority of 1924 in two crucial respects: to restore the powers of the House of Lords so that it could check the extremism of any future majority Labour government, and to move towards introducing tariffs (**144, 155**). Pressure focused upon the issue of extending safe-guarding to the iron and steel industries, but Baldwin ruled this out as a breach of the pledge of 1924. Instead, the major initiative of the final parliamentary session was the de-rating of industry and agriculture, jointly devised by Churchill and Neville Chamberlain. This was a positive policy to tackle unemployment by reducing the costs of all sectors of the economy, without entering the minefield of tariffs. However, it was both complex and dull, proving difficult to get across to the public and failing to arouse enthusiasm [**doc. 18**]. For all these reasons, by 1929 the mood of the party at the grass roots was one of apathy, sullenness and growing frustration: it would take only the right spark to set this tinderbox alight (**132**).

The unexpected defeat in the general election of May 1929 made matters worse, for Baldwin had chosen a platform which repeated the moderation of 1924. The campaign slogans of 'Trust Baldwin' and 'Safety First' were later condemned as demonstrating a lack of imagination and purpose, but the strategy had been deliberately shaped to meet the challenges which the party faced (**154**). 'Safety First' was intended to build upon Conservative strengths: Baldwin's wide appeal, a proven record in government, and practical plans such as de-rating. Although Labour was the main opposition party, the Conservatives were more concerned by the threat from the Liberals. This was not anti-Coalition paranoia: victory in 1924 had been founded upon securing former Liberal votes, but a substantial increase in the number of Liberal candidates would cause many of these converts to revert to their old faith. The Liberal revival was the greatest danger, not because it would lead to a Liberal victory, but because it would let Labour in. Lloyd George's efforts since becoming leader in 1926 were therefore bitterly resented by Conservatives (**169**). Their reactions to his campaign focused upon the stunts and the money which artificially sustained it; the policies were dismissed as reckless, unworkable and knowingly fraudulent. The Conservatives could not credibly outbid such extravagance, and so the theme of honesty and safety was chosen as the best means of turning the tables. Even so, the number of three-cornered contests doubled to 447, and 159 seats were lost. Labour's appeal and acceptability had been underestimated, and the Conservatives suffered especially heavily in the urban districts of the Midlands and the North. The party was left with only 260 seats to Labour's 288, with the Liberals holding the balance of power with 59. Baldwin at once resigned, and a second minority Labour government under Ramsay MacDonald held office from 1929 to 1931.

The period in opposition was marked by serious unrest within the Conservative ranks, followed by a remarkable recovery. From the summer of 1929 to the autumn of 1930 a dangerous gap opened up between the leaders and their followers. The losses in the industrial areas mean that the influence of the agricultural South and of the 'diehards' became stronger within the remaining parliamentary party. Defeat threw into question the strategy of 1924–29, bringing to the surface criticisms of the government's record and hostility towards Central Office. Most important of all, it reopened the tariff question. The pressure for a protectionist policy increased due to two factors: the effects in Britain of the world economic slump sparked by the Wall Street crash of October 1929, and the campaign for 'Empire Free Trade' launched by the press magnate Lord Beaverbrook in the same month. The latter's policy was simply the old protectionist agenda dressed up in an appealing slogan; imperial preference and the food taxes which they required were the keystone of his programme. He had not solved the political problems which these entailed, concentrating instead upon appealing to the agricultural regions and relying on the customary tariff-reform belief that a clear and bold policy vigorously presented would carry the people with it. By the end of 1929 Beaverbrook had progressed from newspaper propaganda to addressing meetings across the country, and in February 1930 he launched the 'Empire Crusade'. This was a separate party which enrolled its own membership, appealed for funds and ran candidates in by-elections [**doc. 19**]. Such divisive competition frightened local Conservative associations and MPs, especially in the safer seats where Beaverbrook's programme, now linked to the diehard agenda of his press ally Lord Rothermere, exerted a powerful attraction. This was crucial, for the threat from the Empire Crusade was based not upon newspaper circulations but upon the fact that it vocalised the real demands of the Conservative heartlands (**132**).

The party crisis of 1930 was caused by Baldwin's resistance to this pressure and by the reluctance with which he advanced towards the 'free hand' mandate to introduce protection immediately after the next election. There were good reasons for Baldwin's caution. Like other Conservative statesmen, he doubted that genuine Empire Free Trade was possible. His eyes were fixed upon the Midlands and the North, for the Conservatives had to regain seats here if they were to return to power. Risks could not be taken, as the unstable parliamentary situation might precipitate a general election at any moment. Advocating food taxes would present the increasingly beleaguered Liberal and Labour parties with an easy weapon, for public opinion in these regions had not yet shed its belief in free trade. Yet as popular readiness to embrace some form of protection increased under the impact of the slump, Conservative grass-roots opinion also leapt forward, and the gap between public and party attitudes narrowed only slowly. The situation was further complicated by Baldwin's poor performance as opposition leader, combining a lack of attack with complacency and inertia, and by his deep dislike for the press lords, which made any accommodation difficult. The tense period from March 1930 to March

1931 was categorised by a cyclical pattern of negotiation, incompatible assumptions, misunderstandings, breakdown and renewed conflict between the Conservative leadership and the Empire Crusaders. The most dangerous phase of the crisis came between the two party meetings summoned by Baldwin and held at the Caxton Hall on 24 June and 30 October 1930. Victory at the first meeting was secured by diverting attention to the issue of dictation by the press: 'as so often throughout his career, playing the constitutional card served Baldwin very well' (**132**). A valuable breathing space was gained but the underlying problem was not addressed, and so after a few weeks the situation again deteriorated. By early October sections of the party in the country were on the verge of openly repudiating the leader, a crisis as acute as that of 1913 or 1922. Just as his position seemed hopeless, Baldwin staged an eleventh-hour recovery, sharply prodded by Neville Chamberlain. Sensing that public belief in free trade was collapsing as unemployment soared, he seized upon an offer of reciprocity made by the Canadian Prime Minister at the Imperial Conference in London on 8 October 1930. This provided a credible pretext for the crucial advance to the 'free hand' policy, without the appearance of any concession to the press lords. At once the wind was taken out of their sails, and the swiftly summoned second party meeting endorsed both Baldwin's policy and his leadership on 30 October.

This was the end of the real danger from the Empire Crusade, but it was not the end of the party's internal wrangling. The final crisis of February and March 1931 had three causes: frustration over the failure to dislodge the discredited Labour government either in the Commons or in by-elections, unrest in the parliamentary party over Baldwin's moderate India policy, and the continued weakness of his leadership. The latter finally provoked a crisis of confidence amongst the shadow cabinet which for a few hours on 1 March came close to persuading Baldwin to retire. Ironically, the intervention of an Empire Crusade nominee in the by-election pending in the ultra-safe seat of Westminster St George's stimulated Baldwin to stay and fight, and forced his reluctant colleagues to rally round him once more. A triumphant success in the House in the key debate on India on 12 March and a heart-to-heart with the shadow cabinet later in the month restored his position. In February an Empire Crusade nominee had split the vote at the East Islington by-election and let Labour in, an encouragement to the stumbling government which provoked a Conservative backlash against those who threatened to divide the party during such troubled times for both the empire and the economy. Against this background, in a straight fight Baldwin's standard-bearer at St George's, Duff Cooper, comfortably defeated the Crusade challenger on 19 March. Together, these two fiascos persuaded Beaverbrook to sue for peace, and his campaign ended with an agreement published on 31 March 1931 (**132**).

With unity at last restored, the Conservatives turned their fire outwards upon the government, led by a revived Baldwin and by Neville Chamberlain, the principal gainer from these events and now the undisputed heir-apparent. The desperate economic position and the spiralling budget deficit meant that even tariffs were displaced from the top of the party's agenda by a higher priority. This was 'economy', and assaults on this front rallied Conservatives at every level as well as striking a chord with traditional Liberal values. 'Economy' formed the basis of common purpose with a breakaway faction of Liberal MPs led by Sir John Simon, and negotiations for an electoral pact held out the hope of combining to oust the government in the autumn – if it did not collapse of its own accord beforehand. The disarray of the Liberal Party and the large swings to the Conservatives in by-elections between April and June 1931 were clear signs that the party was heading for a landslide victory on the scale of 1924. Instead, this outcome was to be suddenly thwarted by the financial crisis of August 1931.

The National Government

On 24 August 1931 the Conservative leaders agreed to form a 'National Government' with the Liberals and a handful of senior Labour ministers, including MacDonald who remained Prime Minister and Snowden who continued as Chancellor; almost all of the Labour Party went into opposition. This new coalition was an emergency measure, and, at the insistence of the Conservatives, its strictly temporary and limited nature was affirmed in the founding document. It was a development which the Conservatives had not desired and it was not to their advantage, for they had nothing to gain and much to lose from an alliance with discredited politicians [**doc. 20**]. They were stampeded into entering the National Government, believing that no other course was open to them. The simmering financial crisis had suddenly exploded during the parliamentary recess, producing an atmosphere of panic in which the bankers' warnings that catastrophe was only hours away were uncritically accepted by almost all Conservatives. Securing 'economy' and balancing the budget were the Conservative priorities. By insisting upon 'equality of sacrifice' they sought to limit increases in direct taxation and to ensure that the huge unemployment bill was not exempt from reduction; in their view both the entitlements and the real value of benefits had become unaffordably generous (**131**). A cut in this area was essential to restore confidence in the economy and stem the alarming flow of overseas withdrawals of gold from London which threatened the collapse of the pound. However, the domestic political effects of such economies could be explosive, and so Conservatives sought to spread the responsibility as widely as possible. They were afraid of provoking class hostility and viewed the inclusion of former Labour ministers, even in the highest posts, as a worthwhile insurance. Less to their taste was partnership with the Liberals, led by Sir Herbert Samuel whilst Lloyd George recovered from an operation, not least because in the special 'war cabinet' of ten this produced an apparent free-trade dominance of four Labour and two Liberals against four Conservatives. The final factors in the formation of the National Government are more controversial: the roles played first by Neville Chamberlain, seen by some as its architect and intent upon dividing and smashing Labour, and second by the King (**142, 155**). The latter was preoccupied by the 'national interest', and decisively pressed MacDonald to remain in office and Baldwin to consent to serve under him; the crucial meeting of 24 August was held at Buckingham Palace and opened with a forceful plea from George V for a cross-party solution. Under all these circumstances, with the imminent landslide and the 'free hand' on tariffs imperilled, the Conservatives could reasonably claim to be making the greatest sacrifice and to be putting 'country before party'.

A party meeting held at the Kingsway Hall on 28 August accepted Baldwin's explanation that there had been no alternative and his assurance that tariffs had been merely delayed and not abandoned. The mood was not one of triumph but of duty and anxiety: the confidence of July had evaporated. During the next two months the temporary National Government evolved into a permanency, as the pressure of events made it harder to risk breaking it up. The crisis escalated and forced the abandonment of the gold standard, and in its place the preservation of the National Government as a stabilising factor became an end in itself. For this a popular mandate would be needed, but disagreements over fiscal policy nearly caused a collapse. Despite a desire to be rid of the Samuelites, the Conservatives needed MacDonald and could not be seen to be responsible for fracturing the lauded national unity. All sides were under pressure to compromise, and the solution was found in the expedient of the 'doctor's mandate' (**153, 132**). This committed the free-traders to nothing, but effectively gave the Conservatives all that they wanted. The party provided by far the largest part of the National Government's MPs and candidates, supported by the most powerful organisation. The October 1931 election reduced the Labour Party to 52 MPs and returned 470 Conservatives out of the 554 victorious 'National' candidates; whilst the scale of the victory was a shock, the preponderance of Conservatives was only to be expected. The party had no compunction in enforcing this mandate for protection, and the Import Duties Bill was passed in February 1932 after the further device of a Cabinet 'agreement to differ' (**156**). It was followed by an Imperial Conference at Ottawa in July and August intended finally to establish the grand preferential design, but dominion insularity and protectionism meant that very little of value emerged. If it had ever been possible, Joseph Chamberlain's noble ideal had been overtaken by the passage of time. Even so, the agreements proved too much for Snowden and the Samuelite Liberals and they resigned in September 1932. However, as MacDonald remained Prime Minister and the vacancies were swiftly filled by the promotion of Simonite Liberals, their departure increased the ministry's cohesiveness without damaging its 'national' appeal.

The National Government of 1931–40 has often been dismissed as a Conservative front, due to the massive majority of the party's MPs on the backbenches. However, this was not reflected at ministerial level, where the minor partners had a disproportionate slice of the cake, including several of the top positions. The Coalition remained cross-party in both complexion and spirit beyond 1935, although by 1940 the departure of all the ex-Labour ministers of independent standing and the increasing closeness of the Liberal Nationals to the Conservatives meant that it had become a mildly progressive Conservative administration which retained the 'National' name out of habit and for the electoral advantages which it might still bring. One reason for the National Government's success was the fact that from the partnership of Baldwin and MacDonald downwards its members worked as a team with much less regard for past attitudes than had been the case in the coalitions of 1915–16 or even 1916–22. The Cabinet committee which framed the 1935 election manifesto included only five Conservatives amongst its nine members, and significantly it did not operate on party lines. The National Government was nearer in tone to the Conservative/Liberal Unionist alliance of the late nineteenth century; in the case of the Simonite Liberals it was also to end in the same way, with a formal pact in 1947 and eventual fusion in 1966.

In its first years the policies followed were clearly distinct from those of a purely Conservative government, and indeed the party's MPs and local activists might have made stronger protests had they not shared in the trauma of the 1931 crisis. The need to maintain national unity was unquestioned in 1932–35, especially as the Labour Party lurched to the left and the Communists and Mosley's newly founded British Union of Fascists proclaimed the coming breakdown of capitalism and the dawn of dictatorship and revolution. In such circumstances MacDonald was absolved of all past sins, and the sensitiveness of the Prime Minister and other non-Conservative figures in the government – which could be acute – was met with unusual if not always perfect Conservative patience. The political, economic and administrative needs of the times meant that even departments headed by Conservative ministers followed policies which embraced a remarkable degree of state intervention (**155**). This was seen in the agricultural marketing boards, housing and slum clearance, industrial rationalisation, regional policy and assistance for unemployment black spots. In the late 1930s the government was increasing spending on pensions, education and road-building, introducing major factory, housing and penal-reform measures, and actively promoting the spread of holidays with pay. However, the attempt to take out of politics the thorny issue of the Means Test and the 'dole' – the transitional relief paid to those who had exhausted their benefits under the unemployment insurance scheme – led to the National Government's most serious domestic crisis. In February 1935 the newly created Unemployment Assistance Board imposed national benefit scales; their apparent unfairness provoked an outcry which led to panic on the part of the Minister of Labour, Oliver Stanley, and their swift abandonment. This incident obscured the improving general picture: after peaking at nearly 3 million in the winter of 1932–33, the unemployment total had been moving slowly but definitely downwards.

The National Government also followed moderate policies in

external affairs, responding to the public mood by persevering with disarmament and paying homage to collective security through the League of Nations even as the international climate worsened after 1933. The influence of the League of Nations Union, the prominence of pacifism, and events such as a striking defeat in the East Fulham by-election of 1933 meant that, due to political as well as economic anxieties, rearmament was proceeded with only modestly after 1934. However, the only serious Conservative revolt to occur between 1931 and 1935 was sparked by the leaders' bipartisan policy in another area: the development of India towards some form of provincial and central self-government (**137**). As India was the keystone of the empire, this was a profoundly unsettling topic for the party of patriotic imperialism. The issue was not a new one: Baldwin's troubles in 1929–31 had been complicated by his endorsement of the Irwin declaration of November 1929, which promised eventual dominion status, and of the Round Table conferences of 1930–32. Baldwin was fixed upon this course for three reasons. First was his personal confidence in Lord Irwin, a respected friend whom he had made Viceroy in1925; second was his fear that India would become a weapon in the party battleground akin to the pre-war strife over Ireland; and third was his recognition that only an agreed British position had any chance of being effective. Like many Conservatives, especially those with recent experience of India, Baldwin accepted that times and expectations had moved on and that the old methods were not only inappropriate but also dangerous. However, this view was not shared by the 'diehards' or by Winston Churchill, who put himself forward in the unlikely guise of their leader. He bitterly resisted the India policy, from his resignation from the shadow cabinet in 1931 through the White Paper of 1933 to the final passage of the Government of India Act of 1935: this campaign sent Churchill into the wilderness for the rest of the decade (**37**, **32**). Suspicion of his motives and the violence of his assaults discredited him. His reputation did not recover from the failure to prove a serious allegation of tampering with evidence made against the India Secretary, Sir Samuel Hoare, in 1934 (**136**). Thus, when he later moved on to criticise foreign and defence policy after 1935 he was largely ignored and had no following in the party.

The revolt over India was never as threatening as the crises of 1921–22 or 1930–31, for dissent never spread beyond a minority of MPs, around one-sixth of the parliamentary party. However, it required careful handling at every stage to ensure that the feathers of the majority were not ruffled, and Hoare proved to be a master of reassurance and containment. Of greater concern was the battle for the hearts and minds of the constituency rank and file. Here the rebels found widespread concern and support, especially in the safer residential seats (where many who had served or worked in India now lived in retirement) and in Lancashire (where the prosperity of the cotton industry depended upon its access to the vast Indian market). Through two front organisations, the 'diehard' India Defence League and the pro-government Union of Britain and India, an often contentious campaign was waged up and down the country. The ministerial side were able to win the key votes in the National Union, but sometimes only narrowly, after appeals to loyalty and with the help of respected senior statesmen such as Amery and Austen Chamberlain (**147**). In February 1933 the Central Council approved the official policy by only 181 to 165, and in October 1934 it scraped through the annual conference by 543 to 520, with nearly 700 abstentions. This was the low point, and when Baldwin fulfilled a pledge to 'consult' with the party before introducing the final Bill in the House of Commons by summoning a special meeting of Central Council in December 1934, he won by 1,102 to 390.

The revolt over India failed for several reasons. There was acceptance that, whatever their wisdom, commitments made during the previous decades had to be fulfilled for the sake of British honour [**doc. 22**]. Battle was therefore joined over the details of reform rather than the principle. The issues were complex, and Conservatives customarily deferred to the judgement of the authorities in such matters. Of particular importance was the endorsement of the government's strategy by the 'men on the spot', the serving and recently returned Viceroys and provincial Governors, several of whom had previously been Conservative junior ministers. The rebels had mainly to rely upon an older generation who were felt to be out of touch with the realities of modern India. Churchill was a source of weakness as much as of strength, and his lead was only tolerated because no other prominent figure was willing to break with Baldwin on this issue. The critics were far stronger in the Lords than the Commons, where many of the 'diehard' MPs were obscure or ineffective. India took up much time and trouble in the early 1930s, but with such a massive Commons majority it was never a real threat to the government's survival. The essence of the debate was the extent and security of the 'safeguards', aspects of

Indian government over which Britain would retain control, such as external policy, the army, the judiciary and the police (**135**). Once sufficient reassurance was given on these points the more lurid claims of the 'diehards' met with little response, especially as the forces of law and order in India restored their control after the agitation and unrest of 1928–31. The India question was often raised in the privacy of constituency executives in 1933 and 1934, but association chairmen generally sought to avoid dangerous tensions and often prevailed upon the movers of excessively hostile resolutions to withdraw them or agree to a blander amendment. Underlying all of this was the simple fact that rejection of the India policy would mean the break-up of the National Government. Very few Conservatives were willing to contemplate this, not least because the Labour Party was committed to granting even greater concessions to Indian nationalism.

By 1935 MacDonald's health and powers had deteriorated, and in June he exchanged posts with Baldwin, who became Prime Minister for the third time. During 1934 and into the spring of 1935 many Conservatives feared that the continuing depression would result in their defeat at the next election [**doc. 21**]. This led to some restiveness over the Coalition and resentment of its forms, such as the Co-ordinating Committee of party whips and the National Publicity Bureau, established in 1934 (**151**). However, unlike 1922 the large majority placed an even higher importance on maintaining the 'national' appeal. There was a final shaky period in the early months of 1935 caused by the visible decline of MacDonald, the débâcle over the Unemployment Assistance Board's new scales, and the final fling of the India rebels. In February 1935 a few of the latter carried their resistance to the dangerous lengths of supporting Winston Churchill's son, Randolph, against the official Conservative candidate in the Wavertree by-election; the result was a Labour gain in a seat which that party had never won before. As in February 1931 this proof of the perils of disunity provoked a backlash which terminated the influence of the dissidents and cleared the air. The nerve of the government was shaken to such an extent by these problems that the Cabinet considered inviting Lloyd George to join, but to general relief Neville Chamberlain vetoed this proposal (**141**). After this the government turned the corner and confidence steadily improved. By the summer of 1935 the recovery of employment and prosperity had become apparent, as had the weakness and confusion of the opposition parties.

Since 1922 the Conservatives had sought to crush the Liberals and restore a two-party system, weighted more in their favour, as the class-based Labour Party would be a narrower and weaker rival than the Liberals had been [**doc. 16**]. The Conservatives had been unable to achieve this in the 1920s but found that the National Government produced just such a realignment. The timing of the election in November 1935 was influenced by disunity in the Labour movement over foreign and defence policy, but the foundation of victory was the economic recovery since 1931 and fitness to govern. The National Government was given the credit for restoring stability and reducing unemployment, and there was no incentive for its supporters to desert it. Labour recovered some ground amongst voters who had stayed at home in 1931 and benefited from a few three-cornered contests, but the government's majority was barely dented. A hundred and fifty-four Labour MPs were returned to face 429 supporters of the National Government, of whom 387 were Conservatives. Between then and the outbreak of war in 1939 there was no evidence of any significant Labour advance or reason to suggest that the outcome of a 1940 election would have been much different, and it is clear that the causes of the 1945 defeat are to be found in the wartime years.

The main problem which the Conservative Party faced after 1935 was not domestic, but the strains of diplomacy and rearmament and the threat of another world war. Only a few weeks after the election triumph, public outcry over the apparent cynicism of the Hoare-Laval Pact – an attempt to resolve the Abyssinian crisis by placating Mussolini's territorial demands – almost led to the fall of the Cabinet and damaged Baldwin's prestige. Hoare was forced to resign, but his replacement by the youthful and popular Eden fended off the storm and the ministry stumbled on to deal with the Rhineland crisis of March 1936. In the summer Baldwin suffered a nervous breakdown, but at the end of 1936 he recovered and handled the abdication crisis with careful firmness. Basking in the glow of public and party approval he resolved to retire after the coronation of George VI, and without dispute the leadership and premiership finally passed to Neville Chamberlain in May 1937. The latter's name will forever be linked with appeasement, but the policy was established well before he became Prime Minister. What was new was the willingness to lead from the front, the extent of his personal identification with the policy, and the degree of determination now applied to solving the problems of Europe. Chamberlain was thought to dominate his Cabinet, too many of whom were regarded as second-rate or as his placemen. Appeasement was for long a hugely popular policy: no one wished to repeat the horrors of the Western Front, with in addition the fearful threats of gas attack and aerial bombing, if it could possibly be avoided. German demands appeared to have some validity, especially in redress of the now discredited Versailles Treaty, and this remained the case until the Nazi occupation of Prague in March 1939 – the first addition of non-German territory to the Reich. Most of the Conservative Party saw no alternative to Chamberlain's policy and backed him wholeheartedly; some in their need for a rock upon which to build their hopes eulogised him and bestowed unquestioning loyalty (**177**). This reached an intense pitch during the Czech crisis of September 1938, in which the real threat of war combined with the high drama of Chamberlain's flights to Germany. Relief mixed with euphoria when Chamberlain returned with a settlement negotiated at Munich, and the atmosphere induced him to the bold but imprudent statements that he had secured 'peace with honour' and 'peace in our time'. Congratulatory resolutions flooded in from the constituency associations, and Chamberlain was supported by all parts of the party, including most of the former 'diehards' – poachers turned fervent gamekeepers.

Only a handful of MPs dissented from this overwhelming chorus of approval, and their opposition was more occasional and less distinct than was supposed by later myth. The origins of the 'anti-appeasers' could be traced to the Abyssinian crisis of 1934–35. Their numbers hardly increased between then and the outbreak of war, and at twenty to thirty they amounted to only a tiny fraction of the parliamentary party. This was the last and least of the four major dissensions within the Conservative Party between the wars, and it differed from the other three in two crucial respects which go far to explain its lesser impact. First, it was based not on the 'diehard' right but upon the progressive centre-left of the party; it did not seek to speak to the Tory bedrock but to floating 'middle opinion'. Second, and perhaps because of this, it found no echo amongst the local rank and file. Here sentiments flowed quite the other way, and instead of being permitted the usual degree of licence, even well-established anti-appeasers were threatened with deselection in the winter of 1938–39. The normal pressures for party loyalty applied still more at a time of national peril, and few of the rebels were attracted by the idea of a 'Popular Front' of anti-fascists promoted by figures on the left of British politics. In fact, the Conservative critics disputed less the necessity or morality of appeasement than which of the pressing dangers threatening Britain and its empire should be resisted and which conciliated, and how. It was this which led to the only moment when the government was shaken, the resignation of Eden as Foreign Secretary in February 1938. The anti-appeasers were further divided amongst themselves over tactics and leaders, and they remained a mixture of 'individual critics and small cliques' (**152**). Only after Eden's resignation did a group begin to develop, but it still lacked cohesion [**doc. 23**]. It was hamstrung by Eden's refusal to attack Chamberlain in public, but was equally determined to keep the rogue elephant Churchill at arm's length. The alternatives suggested by the rebels were either too vague or too militant to command support, and their outspoken language was condemned as a provocation of the dictators. In an atmosphere of near hysteria the anti-appeasers were accused of desiring a war, and this charge was the main cause of the defeat suffered by the Duchess of Atholl when she resigned her seat and fought a by-election in December 1938 (**133**). The critics were unable to extend their appeal beyond a limited circle of inexperienced and in some cases lightweight backbenchers, whose nickname, 'the Glamour Boys', revealed the mixture of resentment, envy and derision with which they were regarded (**177**). Far from threatening the Prime Minister or his policy, it was the anti-appeasers who were under a siege which lifted only slowly as Chamberlain's policy began to unravel after March 1939.

7 Disaster and Recovery, 1939–51

The fall of Chamberlain

The road which led to the Norway debate of May 1940 began immediately after Neville Chamberlain's triumphant return from the Munich conference. Between December 1938 and March 1939 the Munich agreement steadily unravelled: it was soon clear that the pacification of Europe and the settlement of German grievances had not been achieved. There was no transformation in German attitudes or methods, and the pogroms against the Jews and the threats towards the Low Countries increased British distaste and alarm. However, the decisive breach was the Nazi occupation of the rump Czech state in March 1939. This complete and contemptuous repudiation of Munich left Chamberlain and his claim of 'peace with honour' looking foolish and forlorn. The absorption for the first time of non-German population suggested that there were no limits to Hitler's expansionism. The government tried to check him by issuing guarantees to the small states of east and central Europe upon which pressure might next fall, but after this initial flurry they returned to the appeasement of German claims, now focused upon Poland. Chamberlain failed between April and August 1939 to take the steps necessary to turn the guarantees into an effective security system. Crucial to this was an understanding with Russia, but many Conservatives regarded the Bolshevik regime as no better than the Nazi one. The result of this dilatory approach and failure to negotiate seriously was the shock Nazi-Soviet pact announced on 23 August. This paved the way for the German invasion of Poland on 1 September; in retrospect, the last opportunity to deter Hitler had been lost through complacency.

The briefest but without doubt the most damaging incident was the delay in declaring war after the German attack. This was partly caused by problems of coordination with the French, who needed time to prepare against air attack, but it seemed that Chamberlain was making another eleventh-hour bid for agreement at the expense of the victim. His lacklustre and noncommittal speech on the evening of 2 September, 36 hours after the assault had begun, led to fevered scenes in the House of Commons. The failure immediately to honour the guarantee to Poland was felt by many Conservative MPs to be a national humiliation, crystallised in Amery's call to Labour deputy leader Arthur Greenwood to 'speak for England!' (**171**). The debate was followed by a Cabinet mutiny which forced Chamberlain to declare war before the House was next to meet at noon on the 3rd. The coming of war undermined the position of Chamberlain and his inner cabinet of Hoare, Simon and Halifax, for it denoted the absolute failure of the policies which they had so assiduously followed.

Doubts about the competence and commitment of the government grew during the next stage, the 'phoney war' of September 1939 to April 1940. Combined with this was the knowledge that Chamberlain could not construct a genuine coalition, as Labour refused to serve under him, and the increasing feeling that he had neither the record nor the manner with which to inspire the nation during the sacrifices ahead. Chamberlain's own position was affected by the increasing unpopularity of members of his Cabinet, but he would not remove them. During the 'phoney war' Chamberlain missed three opportunities to reshape his Cabinet and refresh its image (**162**). Public and parliamentary support began to slip away. At Westminster three unofficial groups became increasingly critical from early 1940: an 'all-party' committee chaired by Liberal MP Clement Davies, the remaining cadre of the 'Eden group' led by Leo Amery, and a new body called the 'Watching Committee'. Convened by a former Conservative leader of the Lords, the 4th Marquis of Salisbury, it consisted of elder statesmen and senior backbenchers and was intended to give the government experienced advice from behind the scenes. Chamberlain had little time for such interference, and his rebuff, together with growing concern over the direction of the war effort, convinced the Watching Committee that change was essential. The view that the Prime Minister was inflexible and impervious to criticism, and that most of his Cabinet were ineffective and unimaginative, gained ground. In contrast, Churchill, at the Admiralty, radiated determination and aggression, constantly seeking methods of taking the war to Germany. His public standing rose as Chamberlain's fell, and by April 1940 Churchill had become indispensable: his resignation would have brought the government down (**157**).

Two further events contributed to Chamberlain's downfall. The first of these was his complacent assertion that Hitler had 'missed the bus', when addressing the party's Central Council on 4 April 1940. This proved grotesquely ill-timed as it was swiftly followed by the successful German invasion of Denmark and Norway. The failure of British efforts to assist the latter during the next few weeks led to the second and final factor, the narrowly partisan appeal which Chamberlain appeared to make in his own defence during the parliamentary debate on the Norwegian campaign of 7–8 May 1940, calling upon his 'friends' in the House of Commons to rally around him. Although Churchill had played a leading role during the Norwegian campaign and was heavily implicated in its failure, remarkably little criticism was directed at him personally, and ironically the debate led to his replacement of Chamberlain as Prime Minister. For the critics the real issue was not the finer operational points but the attitudes and methods of the government as revealed in the harsh light of the first major clash of arms. Those who defended the ministry missed the point by concentrating upon the incidents of the campaign itself, whilst Chamberlain's opponents on both sides of the House dealt with it generally as final proof of the inadequacy of those responsible for the conduct of affairs since 1931. Errors were blamed upon the cumbersome arrangements under which Churchill had chafed; defeat validated his desire for overall command of strategy. Whatever the real causes of failure in Norway, 'Chamberlain was blamed on the grounds of the defensive and gentlemanly image he projected and for past diplomatic failures', whilst due to his 'fighting spirit and presumed success' Churchill was 'exonerated and rewarded' (**159**). The debate was also about the future, the need for a coalition including Labour which would establish a genuine national consensus and have the authority to mobilise capital and labour, direct the workforce, plan the economy and increase production (**157**). Initially the Labour leaders and Conservative dissidents were reluctant to force a vote, as this would deter waverers and minimise the rebellion [**doc. 24**]. However, as the debate unfolded the strength of hostile feeling on the government backbenches became apparent and forced the adoption of a bolder stance; Davies, the 'Eden group' and the Watching Committee responded to rather than created the critical tide.

By January 1940, 85 government MPs were on active service and many found at first hand that the military deficiencies were far worse than the picture which ministers had been and still were painting in public. The classic example of this disillusion was the decision of Quintin Hogg, Chamberlain's defender in the 1938 Oxford by-election, to vote against the government. Although most of the serving Conservative MPs present at the debate stayed loyal to Chamberlain, 'the sight of sixteen young officers in uniform entering the opposition lobby had a profound effect' (**162**). Thirty-nine National MPs (33 of whom were Conservatives) voted against the ministry and as many again abstained. Only a minority of these were former 'anti-appeasers'; the pivotal role in Chamberlain's fall was played by those who voted against him or abstained, but had no previous record of dissent (**167**). Neville Chamberlain was repudiated not because of any rebel intrigue but as the cumulative result of his own actions during the previous eighteen months. The real causes were the failure of his policy, the erosion of his prestige, his stubborn refusal to alter either the policy or the personnel of his ministry, his personalisation of the issues and his underlying complacency. When the votes were counted on Labour's motion the government had survived by 281 to 200, but even allowing for those absent on war service this was a massive drop in its customary majority. This was effectively a vote of no confidence in Chamberlain, and it was clear that he would have to step down in favour of a Conservative under whom Labour would serve. The only possible successors were the Foreign Secretary, Lord Halifax, and Winston Churchill. However, a premiership in the Lords was administratively and politically unworkable, and Halifax was aware that he lacked the qualities required for wartime leadership. Churchill was the only possible choice, and the famous incident during the crucial meeting on 9 May when, by remaining silent, he made no offer to serve under Halifax simply underlined this fact.

The Churchill coalition

A few hours before Churchill became Prime Minister on 10 May 1940, the German offensive in the west was launched. At once he was plunged into the problems which followed: the rapid collapse of France, the evacuation of Dunkirk, the threat of invasion, and the aerial assaults of the Battle of Britain and the blitz. Italy entered the war, posing dangers in the Mediterranean and North Africa, whilst the U-boat menace threatened defeat in the Battle of the Atlantic. Churchill rose to these challenges, and his pugnacious leadership and inspirational broadcasts stiffened morale and shaped the new mood of national unity and resolution (**32**). In doing so he tapped a well of public confidence which never ran dry; Churchill was the one essential and irreplaceable figure in the government. This did not mean that he was immune to criticism, and at several points his ministry looked more vulnerable than it actually was. However, the difficulties were met by making adjustments in the Cabinet and by securing decisive majorities in votes of confidence in the House of Commons, where every direct challenge melted away.

Neville Chamberlain surrendered the premiership in May 1940 but he remained the leader of the Conservative Party. Churchill and the Labour ministers recognised his executive abilities and the support which he still commanded in the House and in the country. This ensured that Chamberlain retained a strong role in the government, and he defended his own position and that of his followers during the summer of 1940. After this his influence declined, undermined by the revolution in public feeling after Dunkirk and still more by the rapid deterioration of his health from July. He returned to work after a serious operation in September but ten days later was unable to continue; he resigned all of his posts at the end of that month and died on 9 November. Chamberlain's swift departure from the scene could not have been foreseen in May, but the removal of the only possible rival focus of power strengthened Churchill's position. By this time he had acquired a commanding stature as the nation's leader in war and he was the only possible choice to fill the vacant party leadership. Churchill was formally elected without opposition on 9 October, and at the end of December he took advantage of another sudden death to ease Halifax out of the War Cabinet and Foreign Office by sending him to serve as Ambassador to the United States. Halifax was replaced by Eden, whose establishment as the undisputed heir apparent to Churchill confirmed the victory of the 'anti-appeasers' within the Conservative Party not only during the wartime struggle but also for more than two decades afterwards (**38**).

From the autumn of 1940 Churchill's parliamentary position was unassailable. In theory his coalition had the support of every Conservative, Liberal and Labour MP, and there was no opposition in the normal sense. Only a small group of mainly left-wing Labour backbenchers, amongst whom Aneurin Bevan was the most prominent, provided any regular criticism. Apart from this there was intermittent sniping from a handful of disgruntled Conservatives and occasional spells of more widespread restlessness which principally found expression through the meetings of the 1922 Committee. The year 1941 saw a series of military reverses, especially in the Balkans, but the most difficult period for the government came in the first half of 1942. After the surrender of Singapore in February, Churchill deflected criticism by reconstructing the Cabinet and giving a high profile to Stafford Cripps, a popular figure due to his role as Ambassador to Russia in 1940–42. The fall of Tobruk marked the lowest point, but even so the vote of censure moved by the senior Conservative backbencher, Wardlaw-Milne, on 2 July 1942 was easily defeated, by 475 to 25, although there were over 30 abstentions (**163**). However, by the end of 1942 the advance of the enemy had been contained in all theatres, and the slow process of rolling them back had clearly begun with the Allied victories in North Africa.

Doubts over Churchill's direction of the war were muted, but many Conservatives were concerned about the implications of the government's domestic policies. The Churchill coalition revolved around two centres of power: Churchill and his circle controlled strategy and were most powerful in the first half of the war; Labour ministers dominated the key departments on the Home Front, with increasing authority and prestige after 1942. During the period of military defeats and retreats in 1940–42 public attention was naturally focused on the progress of the war effort, in the field and in domestic mobilisation and production. However, as the strategic situation improved, thoughts inevitably turned to the post-war future. Although they were still represented in the government, the majority of Conservatives who had supported Chamberlain felt marginalised and increasingly frustrated. Conservative MPs regarded with suspicion and anxiety the measures of state regulation introduced by Labour ministers, and in December 1941 the 1922 Committee protested to Churchill over this 'nationalisation by stealth'. In May 1942 the Committee successfully orchestrated objections to an excessively rigid and bureaucratic scheme of coal rationing, whilst in February 1943 116 Conservative MPs voted against a Bill enforcing minimum wage rates in the catering trades. Only a few weeks before, in December 1942, the Beveridge Report had been published, to a great wave of popular enthusiasm. The Conservative response was marked by a caution which was completely out of step with this feeling. Objections from within the Cabinet were led by the Conservative Chancellor, Sir Howard Kingsley Wood, and his concern over the cost of the scheme and the burdens it would place on post-war industry were echoed by most Conservative speakers in the debate in the Commons on 18 March 1943. Their negative and uncertain tone sharply contrasted with the unequivocal approval expressed from the Labour benches, and the resulting impression remained fixed in the public mind, with significant results in the 1945 election.

Not all Conservatives were uninterested in domestic issues or detached from the changing atmosphere. The lead was taken by R.A. Butler as chairman of a party committee on post-war problems established in 1941 and as the minister responsible for the Education Act of 1944 (**35**). Butler's efforts were applauded by an even more radical group of Conservative MPs who coalesced in opposition to the party's negativism over the Catering Wages Bill and the Beveridge plan. Thirty-six MPs, mainly from the younger element in the parliamentary party, met on 17 March 1943 and formed the body which a month later became the Tory Reform Committee. The Tory Reformers never became much more numerous, but they represented energy, enthusiasm, fresh ideas and ability. Whilst their assertiveness provoked resentment amongst older and staider Conservatives, in the moribund state of the party they had considerable impact and attracted much attention. In the Beveridge debate their spokesmen marked out a different agenda and called for the immediate establishment of a Ministry of Social Security on the lines of the report. The TRC was active throughout the remainder of the war and their ideas became more widely accepted after the 1945 defeat, but they remained the minority Conservative response to the advance of state control. Other MPs and businessmen more representative of the mainstream of the party and its supporters turned towards libertarian and free-market solutions, in some cases influenced by the argument of Hayek's *The Road to Serfdom* (1944), that planning led inexorably to tyranny. By the final winter of the war the ideological shape of the post-war era was becoming clearer in both home and foreign affairs, where Conservative concern over Soviet intentions in liberated eastern Europe was matched by Labour outrage over British military suppression of the Greek Communist resistance movement.

As a whole, the Conservative Party failed to get much credit for the remarkable initiatives of the wartime coalition, which laid the foundations of a new role for government and heralded the welfare state (**164**). Apart from the Education Act, the measures either enacted or approved in principle included family allowances, universal social security, a national health system, town and country planning, a housing programme and a host of lesser reforms. Keynesian concepts of demand management and deficit budgeting were implemented from the 1941 budget, and confidence in the ability to control the economic cycle led to the commitment to post-war full employment in the 1944 White Paper. The degree of agreement on these matters within the Churchill coalition and the legacy which it bequeathed to the emergence of a post-war 'consensus' have been a matter of debate (**157**, **163**). There was absolute unity on the priority of the war effort, and at the highest level ministers worked effectively together: until the last few months, where friction occurred it was a matter of personality rather than of party. However, the measures passed or promised for social and economic reconstruction marked the limits of agreement, with the most controversial aspects blurred or postponed. The parties were certainly affected by the wartime experience, but they were not transmuted into something different: Labour had not lost its faith in Socialism nor the Conservatives their own fundamental beliefs, and there was much that divided them. Some Labour leaders were attracted to the idea of remaining in the coalition, not least because they too assumed that Churchill's name would carry his followers to electoral victory. Continued coalition was certainly Churchill's own preference, but the pressure from below in both parties for separation was irresistible. From the autumn of 1944 the measures brought forward provoked increasing controversy within the government and in Parliament, and by March 1945 the coalition was clearly on its last legs (**163**). In October 1944 Labour officially announced its intention to withdraw at the end of hostilities, which it did shortly after victory in Europe was achieved in May 1945. Churchill continued in office at the head of the mainly Conservative 'caretaker' government from 23 May until 26 July, when the surprise results of the 1945 general election were declared.

The defeat of 1945

The general election of 1945 produced the second major Conservative defeat of the twentieth century. A total of 393 Labour candidates were returned, a massive majority over the 210 'National' MPs (of whom 197 were Conservatives). The party retained significantly more seats than in 1906, but because it had been largely unexpected this reverse had a more devastating impact. Many Conservatives assumed that Churchill would carry his party to victory, and had failed to detect the ominous signs to the contrary since 1940. The defeat of 1945 was caused by a transformation in public attitudes and perceptions which occurred after the outbreak of war in 1939 and took effect most rapidly between the evacuation of Dunkirk in June 1940 and the victory of El Alamein in November 1942. A range of factors contributed to the parallel development of a negative view of the pre-war Conservative Party and a positive view of the wartime Labour Party. Public shock over the catastrophe of the fall of France was stoked by the troops returning from Dunkirk who told of insufficient equipment, inadequate weaponry and a lack of air support. Recriminations focused upon the responsibility of the pre-war administrations for this lack of preparedness. The leading Conservatives of the 1930s became the scapegoats for every shortage or setback and their reputations were permanently tarnished. The assault upon 'the appeasers' was popularised by polemical left-wing attacks, of which *Guilty Men*, published in July 1940, was the most effective. By the end of that year these attitudes had become deeply rooted, with serious consequences for the Conservative Party in the 1945 general election. The speed of defeat and scale of the peril facing the country transformed the political atmosphere: 'from May 1940 the passions of collective aggression were the main force for change' (**157**).

During the Second World War national resources were stretched to the limit, requiring a degree of government control and popular mobilisation far beyond that of the First World War. Past methods and assumptions had to be discarded in favour of innovation, whilst the 'blood, toil, tears and sweat' demanded by Churchill could only be justified and sustained by the belief that this was truly the 'people's war'. Fair play and a genuine equality of sacrifice on the part of all sections of society were the dominant popular themes, whilst there was constant suspicion that privilege and vested interests were standing in the way. For this reason the levelling effect of rationing was extremely popular; as an acceptable and clearly workable redistributive action by the state it probably did more to prepare the ground for a Labour victory than any amount of left-wing propaganda. 'The roots of class remained untouched, but above ground there was much levelling and trimming' (**157**). The war caused massive upheavals of the civilian population due to bomb damage, conscription and the migration of workers to new industries built on new sites. The evacuation of city children to safe rural districts broke down many social barriers, women were mobilised into war work of all kinds on an unprecedented scale, and even the retired were recruited into Home Guard or Air Raid Precaution units. On the home front the Second World War reached further and changed much more than had the First: it was 'an intensely democratic and egalitarian experience. Classes were obliged to mix in a manner in which they had never mixed before; everybody had to make sacrifices and work together' (**3**). From the desperate period of 1940–42 emerged a feeling of community which had a lasting effect upon expectations of post-war improvements. Pragmatism turned the impossible into the ordinary: state planning and ownership no longer seemed alien or cranky after the wartime direction of industry and labour and the effective nationalisation of much of the transport network. The lessons drawn from these expedients of 'war socialism' at home were reinforced by popular admiration for Russia, seen to be bearing the brunt of the fighting from 1941 to 1944. The mixture of sympathy and guilt with which the Russian struggle was regarded did not lead to mass support for Communism, but the single-handed Soviet containment of German power seemed to suggest that Socialism might be more effective than capitalism in organising society scientifically and efficiently.

The opinion-poll pioneers Mass-Observation found in December 1942 that about 40 per cent of the population had changed their political outlook since the start of the war. The scale and direction of the flow was clear: 'the trend was essentially one towards left-wing attitudes, with the Labour Party as the natural beneficiary whenever party politics revived' (**157**). Whereas the First World War had been a validation of Conservative attitudes and a justification of their pre-war record, the Second World War had the opposite effect. Conservative ministers now appeared to have presided ineffectively over the unemployment of the 1930s, and their party was bound to suffer from the heartfelt cry of 'never again': unlike at the end of the First World War, no one in 1945 regarded the pre-war period as a golden age. As the war progressed, the elimination of unemployment and higher real wages led to a rising standard of living for the working class which reinforced the revulsion against the past and increased expectations of the future. Labour's values now seemed to synchronise with the national mood, whilst the party's prestige was enhanced by its leaders' central role in the wartime coalition.

To many Conservatives the wartime years seemed to be awash with radical and Socialist propaganda [**doc. 25**]. As well as the pamphlets, Penguin Specials and Left Book Club paperbacks, left-wing intellectuals seemed to have captured the BBC and to be constantly publicising their views on the airwaves. The balance of support in the popular press had also suddenly tilted to the Conservatives' disadvantage. During the 1930s the *Daily Herald* had prospered under the joint ownership of the TUC and Odhams, becoming the first title to reach a circulation of 2 million by 1935. It lost some ground thereafter, but shortly before war broke out the *Daily Mirror* changed entirely under new control to become a popular working-class and stridently anti-Tory paper, with marked success as its circulation rose from 1.75 million in 1939 to a new record of 3 million in 1946. Left-of-centre views were smiled upon by the influential weekly *Picture Post*, founded in 1938, whilst during the war both *The Times* and *Observer* shifted to the middle ground under new editors. Press and propaganda normally reinforce existing attitudes rather than subvert them; these changes did not so much create the climate of the times as reflect it, adding expression and impetus. In 1945 the Service vote was particularly hostile to the Conservatives. Many in the party ascribed this to the unsettling influence of the army education service, greatly expanded to relieve boredom and raise morale after Dunkirk. They believed that this and still more the parallel Army Bureau of Current Affairs were riddled with subversive propagandists. However, whilst it is true that most of those with experience of adult education were Labour in sympathy, contemporary inquiries found little evidence of indoctrination. In truth, it was not the teachers but the topics themselves which led the men and women in the forces to question the past and debate the future. At the end of the war, working-class opinion was primarily concerned about the two issues which dominate everyday life: employment and housing. The half-hearted Conservative reaction to Beveridge touched on this raw nerve, and confirmed the fear that promises on these matters would prove as hollow as had Lloyd George's 'homes for heroes' after 1918. In 1945 there was no ideological conversion to Socialism, but, confirmed by the experience of the 'people's war', these priorities pointed away from the timidity and aridity of the Conservative platform and towards the practical agenda enunciated by Labour.

The constant Conservative complaints that the Socialists were not keeping the political truce have to be set in this context, for they were a symptom of the party's deep unease as the sands of popular opinion shifted beneath it. Friction was also caused by the

Conservatives' unrealistic interpretation of the truce, which was only a mechanism to avoid divisive electoral contests and not a vow of silence and abnegation. Where a vacancy occurred, the party which had previously held the seat was allowed to nominate a candidate without opposition from the others, thus freezing the balance of forces as it had been at the outbreak of war. The result was that in most cases there was an unopposed return, but the pact could not exclude independent candidatures, and growing Conservative unpopularity led to some embarrassing and ominous upsets. Significantly, this pattern began with the loss of four safe seats to unofficial radical challengers between March and June 1942. The Common Wealth movement emerged from this as a vehicle for an independent Socialist attack, and thereafter no Conservative or National Liberal seat was free from danger, although there were only four more actual defeats. The by-election record caused definite Conservative unease, but there was an apparent improvement after the loss of Skipton and West Derbyshire in early 1944. The party's difficulties were too readily discounted as freak results due to special circumstances, poor candidates and the venting of wartime frustrations (**163**).

This self-delusion was linked to an underestimation of the real state of the grass-roots party on the part of both Central Office and the National Union Executive. During the wartime period the Conservative organisation stagnated and lost touch with the popular mood; whereas the Labour Party conference was held every year during the war, the Conservatives only met in 1943 and 1945. Patriotic feeling led many Conservatives to treat as improper even the vestiges of local activity such as fund-raising events or branch and committee meetings. Whilst the picture varied from constituency to constituency, despite the pleas of Central Office a significant number closed their offices and wound down their activities almost immediately in 1939–40, and still more drifted into hibernation during the middle years of the war. By 1944, 246 of the party's professional agents had joined the armed forces or the burgeoning wartime civilian bureaucracy, and the membership was equally dispersed on overseas service or occupied by the war effort at home. A skeleton organisation remained, and with some subscriptions still coming in there could actually be a surplus on the local balance-sheet, but for all practical purposes by early 1944 the Conservative Party at constituency level was almost moribund. Allied forces broke out to race across France in the autumn of 1944, and the imminent prospect of a post-war general election led to central efforts to revive the local associations in late 1944 and early 1945. Even so, many had regained little ground by the time the election came, with agents released from the forces often returning only days before the campaign began. Given the advantage which the Conservatives had enjoyed between the wars from their possession of a larger, better-resourced and professionally serviced organisation, its sudden absence must have played a part in the 1945 result (2, 7). Of course the main cause was the change in popular views and expectations of the rival parties, but knowledge of their disarray lowered Conservative morale and compounded the scale of defeat.

In fact the swing to the left peaked in 1942–43, but the pendulum was only very slowly returning and the Conservative election campaign did nothing to quicken it. The party addressed the wrong agenda, and apart from a handful of Tory Reformers the issues which most concerned the electors were given a low profile in speeches and publicity. Churchill's prestige was not as transferable to his followers as had been assumed and his leadership proved to be a mixed blessing. Whilst his wartime contribution was deeply appreciated, his belligerency, age and outlook made him appear unsuitable to preside over reform and reconstruction. The public had expected that he would retire covered in glory once victory had been won, and they disapproved of his reincarnation as a partisan politician. His broadcast of 4 June consisted of a trenchant attack on his recent colleagues which included the claim that a Socialist ministry would be forced to use 'some form of Gestapo' to impose its will; as Attlee was quick to point out, the image of the national hero had been shredded in an instant. However, this speech only confirmed a view which was already widespread: as early as February 1944 polls recorded 62 per cent against Churchill's continuance as peacetime premier. Many Conservatives attributed the confused and abrasive campaign to the 'evil influence' of Churchill's cronies Brendan Bracken and Lord Beaverbrook. As Lord Privy Seal in 1943–45, the latter had urged Churchill to move rightwards and to emphasise free enterprise. The disastrous outcome of the election was instead to place the leaders of the left and pragmatic centre of the party in the ascendant.

Reappraisal, reorganisation and recovery

The defeat of 1945 poured a bucket of cold water over the Conservative Party: the effect was shocking at first, and then bracing and even refreshing. The period in opposition which followed is cherished in the party's memory and has become enshrined in mythology. A picture is painted of fundamental reviews of doctrine and organisation, providing the basis for a triumphant climb out of the abyss. As so often, the truth is much more prosaic (**165**, **161**). The changes in policy were mainly adjustments in emphasis and improvements of presentation, whilst most of the organisational reforms continued established trends. It is essential not to exaggerate the part played by this internal activity: the Conservatives' return to office owed more to the problems of the Labour government than to any action on their own part. This is not to say that the Conservatives would still have been able to return to power as quickly as they did if they had chosen some less acceptable route or had made no effort to modernise their image and recruit a wider membership. However, whilst the Conservative achievement of 1945–51 was neither negligible nor irrelevant, it should be remembered that 'elections are not so much won by oppositions as lost by governments' (**161**).

The 1945 result was the product of an extraordinary combination of circumstances, and once these started to fade then a return to normality in the balance of party support was certain to follow. The dramatic loss of over 200 seats concealed the solidity of the Conservative vote, with Labour taking many normally safe seats by narrow and vulnerable majorities. The total poll of the 'National' candidates fell from 11.75 million in 1935 to just under 10 million in 1945 – unfortunate, but hardly a catastrophe. Recovery on some scale was bound to occur, as the social and economic interests which looked to Conservatism to defend them had nowhere else to go: there was no viable alternative either to the right or, at this time, in the centre. The Conservative Party remained united and still had a strong financial and organisational base: in these crucial respects its situation was very different from that of the Liberals after the First World War. The disaffection of Conservative voters was likely to be transient, as before long the Labour government would inevitably provoke antagonism or anxiety. To bring them back into the fold the Conservatives had only to keep their nerve, avoid appearing reactionary, navigate their way back to the centre and tune up their organisation (**165**). For two reasons reform and renewal met with less resistance within the party than might have been expected. First, the severity of the 1945 rejection rendered the case for change almost unarguable. Second, many inter-war Conservative MPs either retired before the election or stood down as candidates after losing their seats. The consequence of defeat on top of the passage of a decade since the last general election dramatically changed the parliamentary party, not in social but in generational terms, with significant results in its attitudes and receptiveness (**160**).

The reformulation of policy was the most important but potentially most divisive step on the road to recovery. The Conservatives faced three tasks: to recover from the image of indifference to social reform, to rationalise their response to Labour's legislation, and to establish the principles which would define their actions in the post-war world. They had 'to delineate the distinctively Conservative manner in which the party proposed to take over, administer, and improve upon the newly-developed social and economic structure of society' (**161**). Fortunately, clarification and communication were needed rather than radical change. The Conservative manifesto in 1945 had been much more centrist than the Churchillian flourishes and anti-Socialist rhetoric of the campaign suggested. Whilst a Conservative ministry would not have taken the same course as Labour over either state control or welfare provision, the party had claimed credit for the work of the wartime coalition and proposed to extend it. The problem was that the Conservatives were too closely identified with the failures of the past, and their promises for the future were either unheard or mistrusted. The purpose of the policy exercise of 1945–51 was the restoration of credibility and confidence, first within the party and then outside it. Hence 'what emerged was strikingly unoriginal in terms of pure policy but very successful as party strategy' (**2**).

Anthony Eden and Harold Macmillan played important roles, but the key figure in the post-war reshaping of policy was R.A. Butler (**35**). His wartime platform, the Post-War Problems Central Committee, now became a permanency as the Advisory Committee on Policy. As well as continuing to chair this, Butler also oversaw two other important bodies. After its wartime closure the Conservative Research Department was revived, with a youthful new staff including Iain Macleod, Enoch Powell and Reginald Maudling; their work provided the raw material of policy-making, speeches and propaganda (**66**). In December 1945 Butler established the Conservative Political Centre as a means of communicating ideas within the party and revitalising the grass roots. The CPC published pamphlets and leaflets, but its most important function was the Two-Way Movement of Ideas. Topics set by the centre were discussed by the local branches throughout the country at a designated time and their responses fed back up the chain. Despite the appearance of democratic consultation, the purpose was not to shape the party's policies but to ensure their acceptability; this innovation greatly improved communication within the party and may help to explain why the post-war period has never seen internal dissension equal to that of 1918–40. These institutions provided a valuable framework, but despite the later legends the 'backroom boys' of the CRD did not on their own reorient a reluctant party. In fact Butler, Macmillan and Eden were pushing at an open door. Forty-one MPs, one-fifth of the parliamentary party, signed the Tory Reform Committee manifesto *Forward – by the Right* in October 1945, and in the following month the Central Council passed a resolution accepting 'interventionism'. The Two-Way Movement demonstrated that there was no real opposition within the party to the concept of the welfare state, and that 'constituency parties desired above all the weapons to carry the fight into the Socialist camp and were not overly concerned with the finer points of party policy and philosophy' (**4**). Restiveness over the lack of an authoritative statement came to the surface at the 1946 conference and persuaded Churchill that continued vagueness was becoming counter-productive. Shortly afterwards he appointed Butler as chairman of an Industrial Policy Committee, and the result of their work was published on 11 May 1947.

The Industrial Charter was a document of broad principles and not a programme in detail for the next government [**doc. 27**]. It formally accepted Labour's early legislation and avoided reaction, emphasised voluntary cooperation between industry and government, and favoured greater interventionism (**160**). The charter was in tune with prevailing trends, and 'seemed to give the Conservative Party an attractive and intellectually respectable position on the central issues of domestic politics' (**3**). Its reception was carefully managed, with endorsements from different sections of the party, in particular the MPs and the prospective candidates. There was 'a great effort to present what was being done as both original and yet at the same time firmly within the Tory tradition' (**2**). By the time the charter came to be debated at the 1947 conference there was very little opposition, and the handful of critics on the right were routed. *The Industrial Charter* was the first and most important of a series of policy statements, being followed by *The Agricultural Charter* and *Imperial Policy*; the whole then formed the basis of the official programme, *The Right Road for Britain*, published in July 1949, and the manifestos of 1950 and 1951.

There were three key elements in the Conservative programme. First, Keynesian methods of economic management would ensure stable employment and good industrial relations. Second, a wider role for the state was accepted and the party would make no attempt to dismantle the welfare system. Third, there would be no further upheavals or extensions of state power and all irksome controls would be repealed. By the late 1940s many Conservatives no longer saw welfare as inimical to economic success and acknowledged that it could even assist it; they were willing to accept an enlarged state 'if it entailed neither the crushing of private enterprise nor too much redistribution of wealth' (**75, 160**). This shaped the Conservative emphasis upon individual freedom within a communal framework. The distinction was made clear in *The Industrial Charter*: 'Socialists believe in giving people orders. Conservatives believe in giving people opportunity.'

The second task which the Conservative Party addressed was internal reorganisation. Lord Woolton, the popular and successful Party Chairman from 1946 to 1955, aimed to restore the morale of the local associations and to encourage them to be more active in every way. At the 1947 conference he unveiled the 'Million Fund', an appeal to the localities to raise £1 million for the central coffers – a deliberately ambitious target in this era [**doc. 26**]. The money was certainly needed to help with Woolton's expansion of Central Office staff and activity, but the fund was mainly a device to capture the imagination of the rank and file and in the process raise local income levels as well. The achievement of the target ahead of schedule in March 1948 was a turning point in the party's recovery from its wartime atrophy. The second reform also sought to kill two birds with one stone. The report of the Maxwell-Fyfe committee adopted in 1949 introduced strict limits to the payments which candidates or MPs could make to their constituency parties, with the intention of making merit rather than wealth the criterion for candidate selection. This would improve the quality of the parliamentary ranks, and by removing the principal source of large sums force local associations to recruit a wide range of small subscribers and embark upon active fund-raising programmes (**7**). This was the culmination of developments since the mid-1930s, but its implementation was intended to demonstrate that the party was not the exclusive property of the rich. The Maxwell-Fyfe report also established a smaller permanent form of the 'Million Fund', a quota scheme whereby each constituency forwarded an annual amount to the centre based on the size of the local Conservative vote at the last election.

The momentum of the 'Million Fund' was also carried over into a national campaign to recruit a million new members, launched in April 1948. Membership had already recovered from 937,083 in early 1947 to 1.2 million by the end of that year, which was probably still a little below the inter-war level. With this new drive it rose to 2.24 million during 1948, before peaking at 2.76 million in 1950. Equally successful was the new youth wing, the Young Conservatives: by the end of 1949 this had 2,375 local branches and a membership of 160,433. Woolton's own role in all of this was crucial. He had been a popular and respected wartime Minister of Food before formally joining the Conservative Party in 1945. As Party Chairman he had unprecedented prestige; he was a source of inspiration and confidence, an effective propagandist and a highly successful fund-raiser. There was no fundamental reorganisation of the party but rather an elaboration of its structure and a great expansion of its expenditure, its national and local staff, and its ordinary membership (**161**). Contrary to popular myth, the party was only 'democratised' in its internal working in the limited sense of being based upon a larger membership. If 1945 marked the lowest point for the Conservative organisation throughout this century, 1950–51 was the zenith of efficiency and resources. This certainly helped to inspire confidence and enthusiasm amongst the local workers, and thus contributed to the gains made in 1950 and 1951. However, reorganisation had less electoral impact than many contemporaries supposed, and on its own could only be part of the solution to the problems which faced the party in 1945.

The Conservative recovery did not progress as smoothly in Parliament as it had in policy renewal and reorganisation. The defeat of 1945 was a great shock which took some time to absorb, and Churchill in particular felt the rejection deeply. The party was also unaccustomed to being in opposition: the last occasion on which it had faced a radical ministry who possessed a secure majority had been in 1906–10, and then the Lords had provided some defence. Churchill's preference was to stick to simple criticism and give no hostages to fortune, playing for time until the gloss wore off the government. In fact this strategy was largely followed during the next five years, with ultimate success (**165**). Along the way, the frustrations and insecurity of the party over its apparent lack of progress were manifest from time to time in the demands for policy statements or for more effective and committed leadership. An early crisis was caused by Churchill's own role as leader of the Opposition, due partly to his desire to remain uncommitted and partly to his frequent absences from Westminster. Unrest erupted in the 1922 Committee in November 1945, but from early 1946 day-to-day control passed to the safe hands of Eden, who 'played himself in as the unofficial Leader of the Opposition' (**18**). Churchill's main contribution was in the field of foreign affairs and defence, where his pronouncements commanded attention and respect. By returning to the role of international statesman he also recovered some of his wartime prestige and became once again an electoral asset. The Conservatives were normally pragmatic in what they chose to oppose, but over the National Health Service Bill of 1946 they became the spokesmen of the hostile vested interests and came dangerously close to giving the impression of being opposed to the universal principle itself. This area remained sensitive, and in 1949 Churchill made a further blunder, first threatening and then having to disavow a motion of censure on health.

However, by that time the Labour government was deeply embattled and increasingly unpopular. Its problems began with the fuel and food crises of the winter of 1946–47, which were followed by the currency crisis of August 1947. These setbacks shook Labour confidence, and their response to them resulted in an ever closer identification of Socialism with inefficiency, tedium, bureaucracy and 'austerity'. The Conservatives were swift to exploit this, from 'shiver with Shinwell' in the coal crisis to the easy target of the dour Sir Stafford Cripps, Chancellor in 1947–50. The unpopularity of continued restrictions now that peace had come led to popular disillusion. Conservative attacks upon excessive red tape and promises of de-control found a receptive audience, and in 1951 the party campaigned under the slogan 'Set the people free' (**160, 165**). After the watershed of 1947–48 the Conservative opposition had the confidence to move into higher gear, concentrating on economic rather than social issues. An early target was the road haulage Bill, but the major struggle of the final half of the 1945–50 parliament was over Labour's plan to nationalise the iron and steel industry. This was a complex issue upon which the public was at best indifferent, and the Conservatives were able to face a discredited and tiring government with such confidence and vigour that for the first time since 1945 they risked using their majority in the Lords to delay a major Bill. Labour still had the numbers with which to carry the measure and to cut the Lords' suspensory veto from two years to one, but the steel debates were a significant stage in the Conservative recovery, raising both internal morale and public awareness.

By 1949 the Conservatives were aware that they had done all that was in their power to change their fortunes, but beneath the surface the scars of 1945 still remained. The failure to recover any seats at by-elections was a disturbing trend, and it combined with difficulties in the Commons to produce a mixture of panic and frustration in February 1949, after hopes of victory in the Hammersmith South by-election were dashed. Churchill faced criticism at the 1922 Committee meeting of 3 March 1949, but thereafter better results in the London County Council and borough elections calmed nerves, whilst the publication of *The Right Road for Britain* appeased the renewed demand for a clear statement of principles and policy. When the Labour government called an election in February 1950 its plans for further nationalisations had little appeal to floating voters. Aided by the maladroit or offensive remarks of some Labour ministers and still more by the general disillusion with the grimness, regimentation and austere living standards of post-war Britain, many traditional supporters returned to the Conservative camp (**1**). The party made particular inroads in suburbs and made a net gain of 88 seats. However, this was as much a negative vote against Labour as it was a positive popular embrace for the Conservatives, and clearly many doubts remained. Even with the beneficial effects of the redistribution of seats in 1949, the Conservatives had only 298 MPs to Labour's 315. The result left Labour in office, although their overall majority had been reduced to just 6.

The Conservatives were frustrated to have come so close to victory, but could take some comfort from the advance which they had made and the fact that the final distance could be attained in one further effort. The new parliament would give them rich opportunities and clearly could not last for long. In the event, Labour held on for eighteen tense and frustrating months. During this period the Conservatives made a further public commitment which became symbolic of their genuine conversion to a future of active and modernising government. This was a specific target of building 300,000 new houses a year, approved amid scenes of huge enthusiasm in a resolution passed at the annual conference of October 1950. The pledge was ambitious, but it highlighted the area of reconstruction in which Labour had been least successful. In Parliament the Conservatives harried the declining and drifting government with repeated censure motions and procedural devices to prolong sittings and delay Bills. However, their string of minor successes in the lobbies in 1951 was more important in securing Conservative cohesion and confidence than in directly bringing about an election. When this came in October 1951 it was largely due to the exhaustion and splits of the Labour Cabinet. Even with all that had been done since 1945, the outcome in 1951 was still very close. Labour actually secured more votes than the Conservatives, but with 321 MPs the latter had a small but workable governing majority. The improved result since 1950 was mainly attributable not to any Conservative tactic but to the fall in the number of Liberal candidates from 475 to 109, as their withdrawal generally benefited the Conservative candidate.

At the age of 77 Churchill returned to power, and his own instincts and the narrowness of the margin ensured that his ministry followed a moderate line in home affairs. The Conservative dominance of 1951–64 was founded upon this and three other factors which remained constant until the early 1960s: the public appeal of successive moderate Conservative leaders, the growth of consumer affluence over which they presided, and the persistent disunity within the Labour opposition. An effective combination of 'progressive Tory' domestic policy and 'world power' foreign policy characterised the governments of Churchill and his successors from 1951 to 1964. Only after this did a different agenda emerge in part under Heath, with 'Selsdon man' and entry into Europe, and later and more completely with Thatcher's crusade to roll back the state and shatter the post-war 'consensus'.

Part Three: Conclusion and Assessment

Two features stand out from any examination of the Conservative Party during this period: its record of electoral success, and its resilience in defeat. If one word had to be chosen to sum up the history of the Conservative Party since 1900, it would be 'adaptability'. The Conservatives have successfully adjusted to massive changes in Britain's imperial position, in its influence in the world, in the social structure of the country, in the nature and management of the economy, in popular attitudes and culture, and in the workings of the political system itself. Throughout the nineteenth century the Conservative Party was identified with the aristocracy, the Church of England and the interests of agriculture. In the last quarter of that century increasing support from businessmen, in particular in the 'smokestack industries' such as textiles and heavy engineering, had been secured to make it a powerful and effective majority party. Since the First World War all of these social, religious and economic forces have withered on the vine, yet although 'they appear to have been perpetually working against the grain of history' the Conservative Party has gone from strength to strength (**5**). In addition to surviving the collapse of their traditional pillars of support, the Conservatives adapted with conspicuous success to the democratic franchise introduced in 1918. Despite their own fears they prospered and were in power not only for almost the whole of the next twenty-seven years but also during further lengthy periods after 1951.

When the Conservative Party suffered a major reverse, as in 1906 or 1945, the swiftness of the recovery was remarkable; on both occasions it came back to almost level terms with its main opponent in a single general election. In January 1910 a net gain of 103 seats left the Conservatives with only 2 fewer than the Liberals, who continued in office due to Irish Nationalist and Labour support; in 1950 the recovery of 88 seats left Labour with an overall majority of only 6. Although the road back to office after 1910 was littered with pitfalls and delayed by the First World War, on both occasions the Conservative Party returned to command the political scene not just for one parliament but for more than a decade. With rare exceptions the Conservatives have been pragmatic in opposition and flexible and responsive in government; once ensconced in power it has been very difficult to dislodge them. Their infrequent downfalls have not been due to the successes of their opponents but to the calamitous failure of their own policies, sometimes exacerbated by an outburst of faction and disunity.

The continued survival, unity and relevance of the Conservative Party have been the result not of any one factor but of several. The first of these is the nature of the Conservative Party itself (**4**). There is a clear and accepted focus of authority in the role of the leader, who alone defines the official policy. Loyalty is a highly prized value in Conservative eyes and the motto 'United we stand, divided we fall' is emblazoned on the party's heart. For this reason attacks on a leader are often counter-productive, a fact that the Edwardian 'whole-hog' tariff reformers generally managed to remember but which Beaverbrook's Empire Crusade of 1929–31 fatally forgot (**113, 132**). The Conservative Party was not as swift to depose unsuccessful leaders as is commonly supposed, and the examples of Balfour after 1906, Baldwin after 1923 and 1929, and Churchill after 1945 demonstrate this. However, loyalty was not unlimited if the leader failed to defend the principles and interests which Conservatism exists to maintain, or endangered the party's continued existence and effectiveness – the root cause of the events of 1922 [**doc. 14**]. The party has an internal coherence and an integrated structure, cemented by the normal deference of the rank and file to the greater status, experience and competence of those above them. There is a reluctance to question the wisdom of the leadership or the local MP, especially when they were in agreement with one another. The grass-roots membership does not spend much time in political or philosophical debate, having a practical 'let's get on with it and pull together' impatience with distractions and divisions. Constituency officers and members are preoccupied with their own social events, recruitment and balance sheet, topped off at infrequent intervals with the selection of a candidate. The tone has been definitely parochial, far more concerned with local issues than national ones. All this combines to give the leaders room to manoeuvre and has been an important element in the party's flexibility.

The organisational strength of the Conservative Party is the second element in its success. Organisation alone cannot win elections if other factors are against a party, but it can help to minimise the scale of defeat and maximise the margin of victory. Certainly, the Conservative machine must have had an impact in the marginal seats, where elections are in fact decided. Here the swing of even a few hundred votes for or against can be crucial, and an effective and efficient organisation which can ensure that its own supporters poll in large numbers may make the necessary difference. It is hard to quantify the impact of Conservative strength in this respect, as it was a constant factor throughout the period, but the victory of 1935, in which many Conservatives held on with slim majorities to seats which had been won by Liberals or Labour in 1923 or 1929, might have been unattainable without it (**7**). Throughout this period the Conservatives were the innovators in organisation and propaganda and in using new technology, whilst their financial strength enabled them to employ a large professional staff at both local and national level. The redistribution of constituency boundaries also helped the Conservatives in 1918 and 1949, partly because their support was more evenly spread across the country than Labour's and partly because the new towns and new industries which drew population to the South after 1931 lacked established working-class traditions and institutions. Until 1949 the Conservatives were advantaged by plural voting and by the existence of the university seats, but their greatest dividend was the enfranchisement of women. Since 1918 women have provided the largest and often most hard-working part of the local membership, whilst at the ballot box more women have supported the Conservatives than any other party.

The extent of Conservative support in the country is the next significant factor. The party has had a wider geographical and social base than either the Liberal or Labour parties, and this has conferred two valuable advantages. First, the Conservatives have profited from a stronger 'national' identity, which can be contrasted to the 'log-rolling' or 'faddism' of the Liberals and to the divisiveness of the class-based Labour Party. Second, throughout this century the Conservatives have enjoyed much better funding than their competitors. There has been a consistent pattern to Conservative electoral strength. It has been most marked in the suburbs and the arable farming counties: outer London, the Home Counties, the South of England from Hampshire to Devonshire, East Anglia, and rural seats in the East Midlands. To this can be added some other farming districts in parts of Wales, the North of England (especially Yorkshire) and Scotland (especially the borders and the eastern counties), together with

119

the ports and resorts around the coast. Finally, and of pivotal importance, has been the party's record of success in medium-sized industrial boroughs, especially in the West Midlands and Lancashire. The number of marginal seats in these last two regions meant that their retention was essential for victory. The Chamberlain influence kept Birmingham and its environs solidly Unionist and Conservative until 1945, and this made Lancashire even more of a decisive battleground. The loss of Lancashire over free trade broke the back of the party's prospects in 1906, 1910 and 1923, whilst the threat that the India issue might damage the party there caused much anxiety before 1935. In social terms the Conservative Party benefited from the growth of the middle class and from suburbanisation. By the 1920s the Conservatives had displaced the Liberals and become overwhelmingly the party of the middle class, offering an alliance of large and small property owners. Crucially, they were also able to appeal to between a third and a half of the working class on a regular basis as well (**5**).

There were several reasons for this attraction across class boundaries. Not least is the fact that social upheaval is as frightening to those who have little as to those who have much. There has been a consistent popular tendency to turn to the Conservative Party as the 'safe' option in time of crisis: during the dark days of the First World War in 1916–17, under the impact of the economic slump in 1930–35, as war threatened in 1937–39, and – in the person of Churchill rather than the party as a whole – in the Second World War; it is no coincidence that the party's fortunes revived in 1950–51 as the outbreak of the Korean War underlined the emergence of the Cold War. The Conservatives have always done well out of 'wrapping themselves in the flag' and being seen as the patriotic party, strong and determined in defence, and the tarnishing of this image after Dunkirk was especially galling and damaging. In the domestic field the appeal of defensive protectionism was also important. The Conservatives were closely linked to certain sectors of the economy, and in many cases sensible self-interest played as much a part as generational change, social aspirations, deferential attitudes, or working-class patriotism. Conservative values were the third factor in the party's wide appeal, for dislike of change is a matter of temperament rather than of class. One strength has been that the principles of the Conservative Party are a curious combination of clarity and vagueness; what the party stands for is so clearly understood by its supporters that detailed definitions are redundant. 'Policy' has taken various shapes at different times due to external factors, but it has derived from and remained consistent to the same inner core of belief and view of the world. Where it has not, as at the end of the Coalition in 1920–22 or over India in 1933–35, then grave problems can result. This helps to explain the comparative ease with which Conservatism as a whole adjusted to social and political change, and had the resilience to recover from major defeats. This was not merely pragmatism or a desire for power, for in some areas policies grounded in fundamental attitudes were persisted with despite repeated defeats.

The Conservative frame of mind is shaped by individual temperament and by general attitudes and anxieties. Conservatism re-emerges even after apparently devastating defeats, for the fortunes of the Conservative Party have never been bound up in any single issue. The focal point before 1914 was opposition to Irish Home Rule, but this was never the 'be all and end all'. The party had already reorientated itself by the time the Irish question became an irrelevance after 1921, in part to a firm position on other domestic economic and social controversies and in part continuing its close identity with the maintenance of the empire. From the days of Disraeli to the end of the Second World War the party based much of its appeal upon pride in Britain's imperial role, but the Conservatives were able to preside over decolonisation in 1951–64 with comparatively little discomfort. In both cases, although the totems which had fallen had been central to the party's rationale, a substitute was swiftly found to fill the space. In the early 1920s this was anti-Socialism and the defence of private property from despoliation; in the 1950s it was the promise of affluence combined with the maintenance of the welfare state.

The Conservatives avoided the danger of becoming merely a reactionary party, futilely trying to recover a lost past. For this reason they were more successful than their Continental parallels, from whom they differed in several crucial respects. They were always a constitutional party, for apart from an exercise in brink-manship over Ulster in 1912–14 they never became sufficiently anxious or so alienated as to turn to violence (**80, 110, 111**). Since the 1880s British Conservatives have always had the attitude of mind of a governing party rather than that of an excluded group baying from the fringe (**114, 108**). They have had no desire to provoke divisions in society, and in general aspire to a quiet life founded upon national common interest and unity. For this reason, whilst individuals were not free from prejudice, the party

121

itself never sought to exploit anti-Semitism or racism as a political tactic. Defeats normally led not to despair but to reappraisal and reorganisation. After 1923 and 1945 both were encouraged by the leadership and a smooth transition followed; in 1906–11 and 1929–30 factional problems meant that movement in either area threatened the leader's position, and his attempts to freeze the natural processes contributed to internal crises. It was always easier to move with the present and respond to changing issues than secure a consensus for a return to the agenda of the past, as the long-running saga of House of Lords reform demonstrated between 1911 and 1935 (**138, 144**).

Three practical factors constantly pulled the Conservative Party towards the middle ground. The first is commonly overlooked: because the experience of the left is taken as the norm, party activists are assumed always to be a force for extremism. However, much of the Conservative Party's large membership had joined for social rather than political reasons and would have been uncomfortable in any strident or doctrinaire movement; polite and conventional moderation was much more the hallmark of the Tory rank and file. This reduced the stress caused by the second factor: the electoral alliances with sections of breakaway Liberalism which could only be made to work if there was some meeting of minds over policy. For large parts of this period the Conservatives had to consider the susceptibilities of their partners: the Liberal Unionists in 1886–1912, the Lloyd George Liberals in 1916–22, the Simonite Liberals and National Labour in 1931–45. It was not just a matter of the parliamentary seats actually held by these groups; the partnership valuably broadened the base of support for Conservative candidates in the other constituencies. This was linked to the third factor, the magnetic lure of the pool of floating voters. Parties had to motivate and turn out their own customary supporters, but victory required adding to this the larger part of uncommitted and non-partisan 'middle opinion'. There was therefore a potential 'small c' conservative vote which would be alienated by a diet limited to harsh negativism. This was the fundamental problem of Law's strategy in 1912–14, and gives rise to doubts about the party's prospects for victory in 1915 had not the war intervened.

After the advent of democracy in 1918, Conservative governments were even more conscious of the need not to appear reactionary in their outlook. The party deliberately offered programmes which were distinctive in tone and principle from either the Liberals or Labour, but which at the same time would not alienate or alarm middle-class or working-class voters. Moderate and reformist initiatives in social policy were undertaken in such fields as housing and slum clearance. Measures for 'hearth and home', in support of the family and to attract women voters, such as maternity provision and the Widows and Orphans Pensions Act of 1925, were a notable feature of the inter-war years. The principal restraints on Conservative social reforms were a desire to avoid bureaucracy, to avoid too much intervention by the state in matters better left to individuals, and above all a concern over cost. Social measures were regarded as luxury legislation and were always the first to face the axe in a depression, whether wielded by the Geddes Committee during the Lloyd George Coalition in the early 1920s or by the National Government in the early 1930s. Only the combination of political pressure from the advancing Labour Party and relative economic optimism allowed the Baldwin government of 1924–29 to embark upon a much more ambitious domestic programme than the Conservative or Conservative-dominated ministries which came before and after it.

A further factor in Conservative success was the division of the opposition into separate parties, and the divisions within these. The potential anti-Conservative majority was never marshalled into a coherent force, despite the fears of the Coalitionists in 1918–22 or of Churchill in 1929 that this would occur (**30, 122, 132**). However, the Conservative Party did not always benefit from the struggle between the Liberals and Labour. A credible third-party challenge could do serious damage, as was seen in the case of the Labour candidates in Lancashire in 1906–10 and of the Liberals in 1923, 1929 and 1950. The best scenario for the Conservatives was the combination of a weak Liberal challenge, the real prospect of a Labour government, and a moderate Conservative manifesto. In 1924, 1931, 1935 and 1951 in the many marginals where no Liberal stood this meant that the Conservative candidate garnered the votes needed for victory.

The British Conservatives have been the most enduring and effective political party in the world, and it is natural that this discussion has revolved around their strengths. However, there is a danger that these make their success seem too easy and guaranteed. Neither was the case, as the periodic crises and defeats showed. The Conservatives themselves often felt that it was an uphill struggle, and sometimes that their backs were to the wall and their own future and that of all which they held dear was in mortal peril. When in office, Conservative leaders and MPs were never certain of securing continued success; when in opposition, their expectations were often bleaker still. In the immediate aftermath of the First World War the fear of Labour, even of revolution, led to a lack of confidence and to the coalition under Lloyd George. Even after this was abandoned as dangerously counter-productive in 1922, the party remained preoccupied with concern about the likely results of the newly established 'democracy' (**138, 154**). The Conservatives were prone to give credence to their opponents' claims that the tide of history and human progress was running against them, that gradualism was indeed inevitable, and that the working-class voter would naturally identify with the left-of-centre parties. The fickle nature of the new electorate, seen in the 'swing of the pendulum' effect against the party in office, also encouraged Conservative pessimism about the long-term future of the party [**docs 18, 21**]. After each victory, within two or three years there were widespread expectations of forthcoming defeat: this was true after the successes of 1918, 1924, 1931 and 1935, and would probably also have occurred after 1922 if Baldwin had not led the party into disaster a mere twelve months later (**169**). For these reasons the Conservative Party never became over-confident, despite its record of success. The underlying patterns of the period are far more apparent from the historical perspective than they were to the participants at the time, when day-to-day problems constantly competed for their attention. For those actively involved, these affairs were a constant mixture of achievement and disappointment, in which all too often the past seemed unsatisfactory and the future uncertain.

One reason for this was the factionalism and disunity which so frequently obscured the underlying cohesion of the Conservative forces. The longest and most bitter strife was caused by tariff reform between 1903 and 1913 (**85, 87, 113**). It was also the most serious, for it was the only rift to diminish the party's support in the long term and lead directly to electoral disaster. It is notable that none of the other later revolts had that effect: in 1922, 1931 and 1935 the party won victories immediately after bouts of dissension, whilst the connection between the muted rebellion of the 'anti-appeasers' in 1937–40 and the defeat of 1945 is at best an indirect one. Defeat caused unrest, rather than the reverse. The Conservatives found the unfamiliar experience of seeing their opponents on the government benches to be a grating and frustrating one. They were fortunate that only once, between 1906 and 1914, had they to endure the stressful spectacle of a purposeful ministry with a governing majority proceeding to enact fundamental changes to the constitution of the country. Whilst periods in opposition produced one kind of difficulty, periods in office could as easily produce another. Despite electoral successes after the First World War, tensions in the Conservative Party were never far below the surface. Between 1918 and 1940 there were four major outbreaks of internal division and unrest. The most significant of these was the revolt against the Coalition in 1922, after which in descending order of danger can be placed the protectionist struggle of 1929–31, the revolt over India in 1933–35 and the sniping of the 'anti-appeasers' in 1937–40. However, the Conservative Party did not suffer any electoral damage from these rifts. The principal reason for this, and the crucial difference from the Liberal divisions of 1916–24, was that Conservative disagreements were almost never fought out at the ballot box in general elections, and thus the right-of-centre vote was not fragmented. Even between 1922 and 1924, with the unhealed wounds caused by the fall of the Coalition, there was little recrimination in public and no deselections of MPs. This conscious restraint, together with the tradition of loyalty to the party (much more than to the leader) and the horror of division, maintained Conservative unity. Internal rancour was rarely permitted to rise to the level where it could help opponents. This also helps to explain the lack of recrimination after the defeat of 1945 and the swiftness of the subsequent recovery. Tension arose less from numbing catastrophe than when confident or desperate expectations of success were dashed, as with the referendum pledge of December 1910 or the Hammersmith South by-election of February 1949.

The greater cohesiveness of the Conservative Party, cemented by its pragmatism on policies, its concentration on the achievement of power as the primary objective, and the breadth and vagueness of its underlying principles, has enabled it to surmount internal strains with surprising ease. In the last resort party unity prevailed over all divisive tendencies. The free-fooders faced by the 'People's Budget' in 1909–10, the Coalitionists in 1922–24, the protectionists in 1929–31, the India rebels in 1933–35 and the anti-appeasers after 1940 are all examples of the reluctance to cross the final frontier and actually leave the party or join up with another one. The only significant such move presaged the party's worst defeat, when a number of free-trade MPs, mainly Liberal Unionists, crossed to the Liberals in 1903–6 (**97, 103**). Last but not least, luck also played a part in maintaining unity. Joseph Chamberlain's stroke in 1906 removed the only real alternative to Balfour and the only figure capable of leading a breakaway movement just at the point when he was flexing his muscles in a threatening manner. The outbreak of war in 1914 rescued the party from a blind alley over Ireland. The unexpected death of Neville Chamberlain only six months after his fall from the premiership allowed Churchill to become leader and unite the scarred ranks behind him: if Chamberlain had remained as party leader after 1940 a split similar to the conflict between Asquith and Lloyd George which had debilitated the Liberal Party could have arisen when Churchill's stock fell in 1942–43 or after the 1945 defeat. Fortune also smiled upon the Conservatives through the unexpected emergence of the three party leaders who proved to be the most successful of this period: Bonar Law, Baldwin and Churchill.

Part Four: Documents

document 1
Lord Hugh Cecil on 'natural conservatism'

Lord Hugh Cecil was a Conservative MP in 1895–1906 and 1910–37, and together with his brother Lord Robert was the leading backbench 'free-fooder'. The following is the opening paragraph of his classic study of Conservatism.

Natural conservatism is a tendency of the human mind. It is a disposition averse from change; and it springs partly from a distrust of the unknown and a corresponding reliance upon experience rather than on theoretic reasoning; partly from a faculty in men to adapt themselves to their surroundings so that what is familiar merely because of its familiarity becomes more acceptable or more tolerable than what is unfamiliar. Distrust of the unknown, and preference for experience over theory, are deeply seated in almost all minds and are expressed in often quoted proverbs: 'look before you leap', 'a bird in the hand is worth two in the bush', 'an ounce of fact is worth a pound of theory', – these are sayings that express a well-nigh universal conservative sentiment. Novelties, at the first sight, are regarded as new-fangled and either futile or dangerous by the great majority of men. They frighten and irritate, they fatigue and perplex those who for the first time seek to understand them. Human nature shrinks from them and is wearied by them. Men feel that they live in the midst of mysteries; they dwell in the world like children in a dark room. Dangers from the unseen spiritual world, dangers from the unfathomed passions of other men, dangers from the forces of nature: these all haunt the minds of men and make them fear to change from whatever experience has proved to be at least safe and endurable. And change is not only fearful, it is tiring. As men try to perceive and judge a new plan, the effort tires and overtasks their powers. The faculties of judgement and discernment ache within them. Why depart from the known which is safe to the unknown which may be dangerous?

Lord Hugh Cecil, *Conservatism*, Williams & Norgate, 1912, pp. 9–10.

document 2

Scepticism and the limits of politics

After the defeat of 1945 Quintin Hogg (later Lord Hailsham) wrote a popular exposition of Conservatism which has become a classic of the genre.

The Conservative does not believe that the power of politics to put things right in this world is unlimited. This is partly because there are inherent limitations on what may be achieved by political means, but partly because man is an imperfect creature with a streak of evil as well as good in his inmost nature. By bitter experience Conservatives know that there are almost no limits to the misery or degradation to which bad governments may sink and depress their victims. But whilst others extol the virtues of the particular brand of Utopia they propose to create, the Conservative disbelieves them all, and, despite all temptations, offers in their place no Utopia at all but something quite modestly better than the present. He may, and should, have a programme. He certainly has, as will be shown, a policy. But of catchwords, slogans, visions, ideal states of society, classless societies, new orders, of all the tinsel and finery with which modern political charlatans charm their jewels from the modern political savage, the Conservative has nothing to offer. He would rather die than sell such trash, and consequently it is said wrongly by those who have something of this sort on their trays that he has no policy, and still more wrongly by those who value success above honour that he ought to find one. But if he is to be true to the light that is in him, the Conservative must maintain that the stuff of all such visions political is either illusion (in which case they are to be pitied) or chicanery (in which case they are to be condemned).

Q. Hogg, *The Case for Conservatism*, Penguin, 1947, pp. 11–12.

document 3

The advent of tariff reform

Joseph Chamberlain's speech of 15 May 1903 caused a political sensation by advocating the adoption of preferential tariffs with the aim of consolidating the empire as a political and economic force. It was the opening

*salvo in the long struggle over tariff reform which was to divide and pre-
occupy the Conservative Party for many of the following thirty years.*

The Empire is new. The Empire is in its infancy. Now is the time
when we can mould that Empire, and we and those who live with
us can decide its future destinies.... My idea of British policy – I
mean the policy of the United Kingdom – is that here, at the beginning of things, at the beginning of this new chapter, we should
show our cordial appreciation of the first step taken by our
Colonies to show their solidarity with us. Every advance which they
make should be reciprocated.... they are trying to promote this
union, which I regard as of so much importance, in their own way
and by their own means. And first among those means is the offer
of preferential tariffs (cheers)....

If we raise an issue of this kind, the answer will depend not upon
petty personal considerations, not upon temporary interest, but
upon whether the people of this country really have it in their
hearts to do all that is necessary, even if it occasionally goes against
their own prejudices, to consolidate an Empire which can only be
maintained by relations of interest as well as by relations of sentiment. And, for my own part, I believe in a British Empire, in an
Empire which, although it should be one of its first duties to culti-
vate friendship with all the nations of the world, should yet, even if
alone, be self-sustaining and self-sufficient, able to maintain itself
against the competition of all its rivals.

Speech at Birmingham, 15 May 1903 (**19**)', vol. 5, pp. 185–92.

document 4

Tariff reform, imperialism and 'socialism'

*The assumptions behind tariff reform are illuminated in these two letters by
George Wyndham, the first giving his reaction to the defeat of 1906 and the
second the outline of a public speech he was shortly to deliver. Wyndham
had been a Cabinet minister under Balfour and was not a Chamberlainite;
his views reflect the adoption of tariff-reform attitudes by the party
mainstream.*

Wyndham to his father, 24 January 1906
Two ideals, and only two, emerge from the vortex: (1)
Imperialism, which demands Unity at Home, between classes, and
Unity throughout the Empire; and which *prescribes* Fiscal Reform to

secure both. (2) *Insular Socialism* and Class Antagonism. Both these ideals are intellectually reasonable. But the first is based on the past, on experience, and looks to the Future. The second looks only at the present, through a microscope. Between these two ideals a great battle will be fought. I do not know which will win. If Imperialism wins we shall go on and be a great Empire. If Socialism wins we shall cease to be. The rich will be plundered. The poor will suffer. We shall perish with Babylon, Rome and Constantinople. The fight is a 'square' fight. As for the 'Liberals' and 'Unionist Free Traders' – the 'Whigs' of our day – Well! Their day is over. It is they who are drowned. The Imperialists and Socialists emerge. That is the dividing line of future parties.

Wyndham to Hanson, 19 December 1907
Tomorrow I shall try something like this.... There are only 2 plans, Socialistic and Imperialistic. Look at first. Increase direct taxation and rates, to feed and clothe the child and to pension his parents. Borrow money to build them a better and more expensive house. What happens? Higher taxes drive capital abroad. Higher rates prevent erection of factories and workshops, etc., etc. Ends in turning England into the Poplar and West Ham of Europe. The plan is bad, because you tried to find out *How* to remedy the evil, without asking, first, *Why* it is there. Why was the child hungry? Because his father was *unemployed*. Why? Because of
  Pauper aliens
  Dumped goods
  Sweated goods
  High rates
  High direct taxes.
And into it I go with gusto and glee, and work right up the keyboard to the crashing harmonies of Empire and Employment with a lovely leit-motif of the 'Sister States' – bless 'em – carolling like birds through the strumming of Statistics and bugle-calls of the higher Patriotism.

J.W. McKail and G. Wyndham, *Life and Letters of George Wyndham*, Hutchinson, 1925, vol. 2, pp. 540, 594–6.

document 5
The 'food tax' bogey

The 'food tax' aspect of tariff reform was a heavy electoral burden, but the 'whole-hoggers' would not accept this. They remained convinced that half-hearted advocacy on the part of leaders and candidates led to defeat and that the policy only needed to be presented boldly for it be an election winner.

Tariff Reform was our trump card. Where we won, we won on and by Tariff Reform. Even where we lost, it was the only subject in our repertoire about which people really cared.... The Food Taxes were, of course, the great difficulty our men met with. On the whole those who faced this difficulty most boldly came off best. But *where the question of food taxation had been shirked or evaded BEFORE the contest, it loomed largest IN the contest.* It requires time and repetition to beat down the cry of dear food, 'black bread and horse-flesh', and to make the people look at the question in the proper light as first and foremost, for working-men, one of employment. But it can be done if once our candidates see that they must do it, if they acquire for themselves and impart to others the necessary information, and deal with this question in frequent speeches, not waiting to be challenged upon it but going to meet the enemy in the gate. The ignorance of their own case shown by many of our candidates was shocking.... Where a man has become a convinced Tariff Reformer, nothing will shake him. It is a religion and he becomes its ardent missionary. These are our best workers.

Austen Chamberlain to Balfour, 29 January 1910, Sir A. Chamberlain, *Politics from Inside: An Epistolatory Chronicle 1906–14*, Cassell, 1936, pp. 196–7.

document 6

The decision to reject the 'People's Budget', 1909

The decision of the Conservative leader in the House of Lords, Lord Lansdowne, to throw out Lloyd George's 1909 budget was considered and not intemperate; the reasoning set out in this letter to a senior colleague mixed shrewd foresight with too complacent a conclusion.

... I am in favour of rejection, upon the broad ground that the Finance Bill is a new departure of the most dangerous kind, to which the House of Lords has no right to assent until it is sure that HMG have the support of the country. This, so far as I am able to make out, is the feeling of most of our friends, although there are no doubt some dissentients. Those who think as I do, do not conceal from themselves that the Budget is probably not unpopular with the working classes, or, at any rate, with a considerable section of those classes. I do not like the reports from Scotland; from other parts of the country they are less disquieting. We must, I think, assume that, if there is a general election, we may be beaten at the polls; but to my mind the consequences of acquiescing in a measure which we know to be iniquitous, and have denounced as such, would be more deplorable than the consequences of a defeat.... in such an event, the position of the H. of L. would have been gravely and permanently impaired. We could never in future, however outrageous the financial policy of a Radical Government might be, claim the right to stand in its way.

I think it, then, conceivable that we shall be defeated, but I take it as certain that the Radical majority would be greatly decreased. This would be to some extent a justification of our conduct, and we should be far stronger if we were no longer a mere handful in the House of Commons. If the majority either way is to be a *small* one, it would, I think, be better for us to be in a large minority than in a small majority.

Your fear is that such a defeat would involve the virtual destruction of the H. of L. as a Second Chamber.... But the destruction of the House of Lords is not to be accomplished in a few weeks or months; and when the heat and fury of the general election has spent itself, the country will, I believe, be quite able to discriminate between the two issues – and I do not believe the country desires a Single Chamber system. By the time the H. of L. issue is ripe for treatment, the popularity of the Budget will, unless I am mistaken, have greatly diminished. We shall not, in my opinion, get through the present crisis without two general elections.

Lansdowne to Balfour of Burleigh, 2 October 1909, in Lord Newton, *Lord Lansdowne*, Macmillan, 1929, pp. 378–9.

document 7

The passage of the Parliament Act

The Liberal government's Bill to reduce the powers of the House of Lords aroused great passion amongst Unionist politicians and provoked further disunity. Lansdowne recommended abstention, whilst some Unionists decided to vote for the Bill in order to avoid the threatened mass creation of new peers. The former Lord Chancellor, Halsbury, became the rallying point for those determined to resist to the bitter end: George Wyndham, one of several 'die-hards' in the shadow cabinet, gives the flavour of their apocalyptic mood.

There is a fierce indignation against those who threaten to vote with the Government against their own convictions, for the sole purpose of preventing the creation of peers at all costs, including the cost of a general acquiescence in a policy which the majority of Englishmen believe to be disastrous. That indignation will burn up the Unionist Party if this outrage is committed. . . .

There is a strong feeling that Lord Lansdowne ought to restore liberty of action to men whose consciences are wounded by what he asks them to do, and that he ought to denounce the project of any Unionist Peer voting with the Government.

Those of us who act with Lord Halsbury will not yield to any pressure. . . . if we withhold our list those who say they will vote with the Government must discover for themselves the exact number of 'black-legs' needed to consummate the ruin of the House of Lords and destroy the constitution for ever. We are not going to measure the margin of treachery required to complete so infamous an act. They must attempt that nauseous task unaided save by the authors of the Revolution and the Harmsworth press. We believe that they cannot effect their purpose and are determined to defeat it.

Wyndham to Ward, 30 July 1911, J.W. McKail and G. Wyndham, *Life and Letters of George Wyndham*, Hutchinson, 1925, vol. 2, pp. 697–8.

document 8

The departure of Balfour, 1911

Aware that Balfour intended shortly to announce his resignation, the Chief Whip, Lord Balcarres (heir to the Earl of Crawford), penned this review of his qualities and the problem of finding an adequate replacement.

This afternoon his criticism of the government proposals for dealing with their programme was overwhelming. I heard many members say that no more formidable indictment was conceivable. . . . He seems so indispensable to the party, and his merits are so fully acknowledged that even if he abandoned the leadership tomorrow nobody could allege that an alteration was demanded by the party in consequence of defective power or intellect. He stands supreme in our ranks. . . . It is well that the successor should have to win his spurs and realise the power of his predecessor. This will stimulate the activity of our new leader.

Who shall he be? For my part I can look only to Austen Chamberlain. Walter Long is hopeless, impossible. He is stale and turgid: his temper is peppery and twelve months hence will be uncontrollable. Bonar Law won't do. He seems almost to be retiring from politics so sporadic is his attendance, and so reluctant is he to take an active part in our work. Moreover he is more reserved and unapproachable every day. Wyndham is too flighty, Alfred Lyttelton too sentimental, F.E. Smith too inexperienced, Harry Chaplin fifty years too old – and so forth.

Balcarres (Crawford) diary, 25 October 1911 (**181**), p. 237.

document 9
Lancashire and the crisis of tariff reform, 1912–13

Bonar Law and Lansdowne's announcement at the end of 1912 that Balfour's referendum pledge on food taxes of 1910 no longer applied provoked a storm in the Unionist Party which threatened to lead to both leaders' departure. The most vehement hostility came from Lancashire, where the leading figure, Lord Derby, had presided over a seething meeting of the county organisation.

The position is very serious. As you know I warned the Shadow [cabinet] what the effect of withdrawing the referendum pledge would be, and matters are really worse than I anticipated. There was absolute unanimity in the meeting. They are quite determined that they will not have Food Taxes – some of them, a majority I think, wanted to throw over Tariff Reform altogether. I wanted to adjourn for six weeks, but they would not do so for more than three weeks. On January 11 we shall pass a resolution calling upon Bonar Law to give us some guarantee that there should be some appeal to the country before Food Taxes are imposed. It would be useless to try and stop them. Moreover I entirely agreed with them. This matter cannot be hushed up, nor in my opinion is time of any value. If we had had this out after 1906 we should be in a much better position now. I am not going to be browbeaten by the food taxers any more, they have persistently ignored the fact that Lancashire hates Tariff Reform, and have paid no respect to our wishes in this subject. They are going to learn that they have to. A split seems to me inevitable, unless the food taxers give way.

Derby to Long, 25 December 1912 (**26**), pp. 176–7.

document 10
Home Rule and the resistance of Ulster, 1912–14

Under Bonar Law's leadership the Unionists adopted an intransigent public posture against the Irish Home Rule Bill, the weak point of which was the vehement opposition of the Protestant counties of Ulster.

This is what Bonar Law has said:
1. The Unionist Party is pledged, if Government persist in carrying their Bill unmodified without an appeal to the people, to support Ulster in its resistance.
2. That support does not mean merely making speeches but any and every measure that might be effective to prevent the coercion of Ulster.
3. That pledge rests on *the whole body of Unionists* (seeing that they have at meeting after meeting enthusiastically endorsed it), and not merely on the party leader.

 . . . There are a great many people who still entirely fail to realise, what the strength of our feeling is on this subject. They think it is just an ordinary case of opposition to a political measure, a move in the party-game. And so it may be to a great many Unionists, but there is certainly a large body, who feel that the crisis altogether transcends anything in their previous experience, and calls for action, which is different, *not only in degree, but in kind*, from what is appropriate to ordinary political controversies.

Milner to Selborne, 18 February 1914 (**172**), pp. 102–3.

document 11
The problem of patriotic opposition

When war broke out in 1914 the Liberal government remained in office, leaving the Conservative opposition in a position of frustration and difficulty. By January 1915 the shadow cabinet was debating which course to follow; the possibility of coalition was considered but not generally desired.

We are expected to give a mute and almost unquestioning support to everything done by the Government, to maintain a patriotic silence about the various blunders that have been committed in connection with the War . . . to dismantle our Party machinery, to forgo all possibility of Party advantage, and to allow, without a protest, the most outrageously partisan of measures, such as the Plural Voting Bill, to be carried over our heads, or even with our consent. In other words, the Government are to have all the advantages, while we have all the drawbacks of a coalition. They tell us nothing or next to nothing of their plans, and yet they pretend our Leaders share both their knowledge and their responsibility. . . . The whole agency of the Unionist Party has been utilised to obtain additions to the Army. But if we ask how the effort has fared, or what is the present situation, we are treated almost as though we were enemies of our country.

I do not think that this state of affairs can continue indefinitely, both because the temper of our Party will not long stand it and because, in the interests of the Nation, the position is both highly inexpedient and unfair. We are ready enough to give the Government our support, but it can only be if they give us their confidence, and if they refrain from taking advantage of our patriotism. We cannot cease to be an opposition for our own purposes, and yet remain one for theirs. The question is what steps, if any, should be taken to terminate this situation? Like Mr Long, I am entirely against a Coalition Government, even if, (which I do not think at present is the least likely) it were proposed to us by the other side. A Coalition would tie our hands and close our lips even more effectively than at present.

Curzon's memorandum to the shadow cabinet, January 1915 (**172**), pp. 124–5.

document 12
The continuation of the Lloyd George Coalition, 1919

The continuation of the wartime Coalition was not controversial within the Conservative Party in the immediate post-war period. Its success revolved around the relationship between Bonar Law and Lloyd George, as this extract from the diary of William Bridgeman, a junior minister, shows.

The P.M. who returned on June 28 from Paris gave a dinner to members of the Govt . . . . Ll. George gracefully commended and thanked us for doing so much work in his absence, paid a very fine tribute to B. Law for his loyalty . . . & drank B.L.'s health.

B. Law said he had begun by being frightened of L.G. whose career alarmed a cautious Scot like himself, but that now he knew him well, he realised what magnificent qualities he had, especially vitality & endurance. He said he regarded his position in this coalition as different from the last, and refused the role of trying to drive as hard a bargain for his party as he could. He echoed L. George's call for unity. . . .

It was an interesting evening – very hilarious at times – & all really glad to have the P.M. back at home, & much affected by the glamour of his extraordinary personality.

Bridgeman diary, 4 July 1919 (**182**), pp. 140–1.

document 13

The problems of Austen Chamberlain, 1921–22

By the beginning of 1922 the Coalition was becoming increasingly unpopular amongst Conservative MPs and local associations. The new leader, Austen Chamberlain, contemplated the results when in January the Party Chairman, Sir George Younger, publicly denounced the idea of an immediate election and enraged Lloyd George and F.E. Smith (now Lord Birkenhead).

I know what I want. My colleagues are agreed with me and Younger intends to carry out my policy; yet they all seem to conspire to prevent it. Younger humiliates the P.M. publicly, F.E. attacks Younger personally; Bonar Law tries on the crown, but can't make up his mind to attempt to seize it, won't join us and share the load, but watches not without pleasure the troubles of his friends, and the Die-hards, instead of responding to my advances, harden in their resistance.

Austen Chamberlain to his sister, 26 February 1922, in Sir C. Petrie, *The Life and Letters of the Right Hon. Sir Austen Chamberlain*, Cassell, 1940, vol. 2, p. 181.

document 14

The fall of the Coalition, 1922

By the autumn of 1922 the party was clearly hostile to entering an election committed to continuing the Coalition in its existing form. When the leading Coalitionists met at Chequers and resolved to rush the election and thereby avoid consulting MPs or the National Union, this provoked a revolt in which Younger and his deputy, Sir Robert Sanders, played key roles.

The fat is properly in the fire if our mandarins persist in the policy which they appear to have adopted at Chequers. I am to see Austen tomorrow afternoon, and shall let him distinctly understand that such a policy amounts to an inevitable split in the party; that he is not justified in making any public declaration on the subject until he has consulted the whole of his Ministers, senior and junior; and that also the party ought to be given an opportunity of expressing its view before anything is finally settled. He may not like this but I shall insist upon it.

After all he is only Leader in the House of Commons, but even if he were Leader of the party, it is his first duty to try to preserve party unity, and to adopt a policy which he knows perfectly well will rend us in twain, without at all events taking steps to ascertain that the great majority of the party is behind him, would be, in my opinion, an outrage. I certainly could not be the instrument for carrying out any such policy, and I am very glad to see that your view clearly coincides with my own.

I hope there may yet be time to avert the catastrophe which threatens us. I am writing quite shortly, and I am glad to tell you that Leslie Wilson [the Chief Whip] is completely in accord with me, and has written Austen in no uncertain terms as to his own position. It is, as you say, a damnable mess, and I have lost all confidence both in the Government and in the lot who represent us in the Cabinet.

Younger to Sanders, 25 September 1922 (**179**), pp. 183–4.

document 15
The aftermath of the tariff election, 1923

The 1923 defeat was followed by several weeks of feverish intrigue. However, Derby and the former Coalitionists misread the feelings of the party, which preferred Labour in office to any revival of coalition.

Our great leader has indeed led us to disaster, and the landslide which I was always a little afraid of but had hoped might be avoided has come.... it makes one very bitter, knowing how unnecessary the whole thing was. But it is no use crying over spilt milk and the question is, what are we to do now? Our majority has gone . . . and then the great question is, which is the second party? If it is Labour, Baldwin after resigning will probably advise the King to send for Ramsay MacDonald, and to my mind, that would be absolutely fatal, as I believe he might be able to get a working agreement with the Liberals, and the Conservative Party would cease to exist. On the other hand, if Baldwin could be persuaded to resign, always supposing we are the largest Party, and ask the King to send for somebody in our Party to see if he could form a Government, why should not you or Austen take it and see if you could not come to an agreement with Lloyd George for a Coalition Government? There would have to be concessions on both sides. . . . There would be no fear of any Die-Hards opposing a Coalition now that they see what they have brought us, and there will be no more trouble in that direction.

Derby to Birkenhead, 7 December 1923 (**26**), p. 541.

document 16
Three-party politics in the 1920s

Others interpreted the outcome in 1923 in a quite different way: here the leading protectionist, Cabinet minister Leo Amery, sums up the anti-Coalitionist outlook and strategy throughout the decade.

Found Willie Bridgeman at his office and heard that Stanley [Baldwin] was thinking of resigning both the Premiership and the Leadership of the Party. We agreed that he ought not to do either, least of all the latter. . . . dashed off a strong appeal to Stanley urging him to realise that he stood head and shoulders above any man in the country and that if he now threw up the sponge he would cart all of us who had pinned our faith to him and would smash the Party. I also pressed him to stay on and meet the House so as to state the issue in his own way and force the Liberals to face the necessity of supporting Labour which is bound to mean their eventual break-up and disappearance as a Party. My whole object in this and subsequent talks and letters has been to convince him that our main object in the immediate future is the destruction of the Liberal Party and the absorption of as much of the carcass as we can secure – this in opposition to all the born idiots, from Austen and F.E. downwards, who are clamouring for us to support an Asquith Government which would mean the final break-up of our Party. One of the three parties has to disappear and the one that is spiritually dead and has been so for thirty years or more is the natural victim.

Amery diary, 8 December 1923 (**170**), p. 361.

document 17

Baldwin and the 'New Conservatism'

Baldwin's appeal to his party not to support the Bill attacking the trade-union political levy proposed by diehard MP F.A. Macquisten in March 1925 was a parliamentary triumph which established his authority; it was also a classic statement of the aims and tone of his 'New Conservatism'.

For two years past, in the face of great difficulties, perhaps greater than many were aware of, I have striven to consolidate, and to breathe a living force into my great Party.... we believe in the justice of this Bill which has been brought in today, but we are going to withdraw our hand, and we are not going to push our political advantage home at a moment like this. Suspicion which has prevented stability in Europe is the one poison which is preventing stability at home, and we offer the country today this: we, at any rate, are not going to fire the first shot. We stand for peace. We stand for the removal of suspicion in the country. We want to create an atmosphere, a new atmosphere in a new Parliament for a new age, in which the people can come together. We abandon what we have laid our hands to. We know we may be called cowards for doing it. We know we may be told that we have gone back on our principles. But we believe we know what at this moment the country wants, and we believe it is for us in our strength to do what no other party can do at this moment, and to say that we at any rate stand for peace.

I know, I am as confident as I can be of anything, that that will be the feeling of all those who sit behind me, and that they will accept the Amendment which I have put down in the spirit in which I have moved it. And I have equal confidence in my fellow countrymen throughout the whole of Great Britain. Although I know that there are those who work for different ends from most of us in this House, yet there are many in all ranks and all parties who will re-echo my prayer: 'Give peace in our time, O Lord.'

House of Commons Debates, 6 March 1925, 5th series, vol. 181, cols 833–41.

document 18
The decline of the second Baldwin government, 1927–29

The state of opinion in the parliamentary Conservative Party during the final months of the 1924–29 ministry is preserved in the diary of Cuthbert Headlam, a junior minister with a highly marginal seat in the industrial North-east.

4 November 1928: . . . but for the unemployment I should feel fairly confident – but unemployment is a dreadful snag and one can quite realise that people may argue that things can't be worse and may be better as the result of a change of Government. Sometimes, indeed, I wonder why there are any Conservatives in an industrial area: the promises made by the Socialists must be so entrancing to the people who are poor and suffering. It is a huge tribute to English common sense that they are not taken at their face value.

8 November 1928: I find everyone at the HofC in a somewhat gloomy state – our people almost as a body seem to think that we are going to take a toss at the next election – apparently the opposition to the de-rating bill is more widespread than I imagined. It is too complicated and revolutionary a series of proposals to be popular however good its effects may be going to be – and of course a lot of interested people – [Poor Law] Guardians, small officials, etc., are doing all they can to throw cold water on the Government's proposals.

Headlam diary, 4 and 8 November 1928 (**169**), p. 156.

document 19
The Empire Crusade and the crisis of 1930

Lord Beaverbrook's 'Empire Crusade' campaign for the adoption of a full tariff programme posed considerable dangers between February and October 1930. This memorandum from the Principal Agent, Robert Topping, to the Party Chairman, J.C.C. Davidson, was written several months before the crisis peaked.

The happenings within the Party organisation since Easter have been so extremely disturbing that I feel compelled to tell you that, in my view, the position is most serious.... Our 'Home and Empire' campaign is not going at all well. There is a slackness throughout the whole organisation. The constituencies are disinclined to follow our lead. Representations are reaching us daily from persons suggesting we should adopt Beaverbrook's full policy of Empire Free Trade, and altogether there exists an air of uneasiness and unrest that alarms me. At present I greatly fear grave dissension in the Party.

The present position is, I think, due to a series of misunderstandings in the minds of our supporters.... I quite appreciate how important it was to secure Beaverbrook's support if possible, but I am absolutely certain it will ruin our chances of success at the next general election if the impression gets abroad that the policy of the Party may be altered from day to day to suit the whims of Beaverbrook.

Memo from the Principal Agent to the Chairman, 2 May 1930 (**176**), pp. 335–6.

document 20
The formation of the National Government, 1931

In the summer of 1931 the second Labour government was tottering and an economic and political crisis clearly approaching. The Conservatives expected to take office themselves and did not favour the idea of a cross-party 'National Government', as this letter written after a shadow cabinet debate shows.

The question you put to us was 'What did we think you should do if they ask you to join in forming a National Government under Ramsay MacDonald?' My own opinion is that you should refuse unhesitatingly, but offer to give them all support. The position is entirely unlike the War, when all decent people of all parties were at one as to the object and there was no division on Party lines as to the measures to attain it. I believe that joining a National Government would mean entanglement with the Socialists and that it would be very difficult later to disengage. Bad in any case, it will be made infinitely worse by the presence of Lloyd George.... If, however, you refuse to join a National Government under MacDonald – and I gather this is also your own view – it is necessary to consider what would happen next.

1. The Government might carry on with the promise of your support....

2. They might dissolve or resign. In the latter case, to get support enough to carry the necessary measures, I expect you would have to go to the country. Result in either case – a General Election super-added to the crisis. I am sure you would win, but of course it would have this disadvantage, that the country would not have learned its lesson, and the Socialists would join in attacking you for the very measures you took to meet the crisis.

3. The pressure of public opinion to form a National Government might grow so strong that you might find it difficult, despite your own views, to persist in refusing. If they would make you the head of the Government, that might make the proposal more acceptable, but I do not think they would do this. In this event, I think you would stipulate for a neutral Prime Minister, if such a man could be found and would consent, and for a moratorium for all measures other than those directly dealing with the crisis. When the crisis was surmounted, he would retire. Under such circumstances the Party could disengage; an election would almost certainly follow, and you would come by your own. The extent to which the country learned its lesson would depend upon the degree to which the causes of the trouble were made plain to the public, and upon the acquiescence by whatever Socialists were included in the Government in the measures which were taken.

Steel-Maitland to Baldwin, 28 July 1931, Steel-Maitland MSS, Scottish Record Office, GD 193/94/2/179–181.

document 21

The future of the National Government,1934–35

Cuthbert Headlam, a junior minister in 1926–29 and 1931–34, reflects upon the position of the National Government after two and a half years in office; like many Conservatives, he accepted it but was not an uncritical enthusiast. The extract illustrates typical Conservative pessimism about the government's prospects, and more generally about the nature of the democratic electorate.

The position of the Government in the House seems to me to be perfectly secure: it arouses no particular enthusiasm amongst its supporters, but none of them is at all anxious to cabal against the present regime – principally because there is no one except Winston [Churchill] to lead anything in the nature of a revolt. There is also a feeling amongst a lot of these unfledged politicians that it is only by maintaining the 'Nat. Govt.' in power and appealing to the country again on what they choose to call 'a non-party' basis that they will be able to retain their seats – one finds in conversation that this idea is in the minds of a lot of people who realise well enough that there is nothing behind the Nat. Govt. façade and that really and truly there are practically no Nat. Lab. or Nat. Lib. voters in the country – I am afraid that these people may be in for a nasty disillusionment when the General Election comes along. The one and only hope for a satisfactory result on Nat. Govt. ticket is that the election may come along at a time of crisis – or that we may succeed in catching the popular fancy by some piece of luck a few weeks before the intelligent electors have their say – we certainly shan't gain their support for what we have done for them so far.

Headlam diary, 30 April 1934 (**169**), p. 302.

document 22

The revolt over India

The problems faced by the India rebels of 1933–35 are indicated in the letter from Sir Henry Cautley, MP for East Grinstead 1910–36, to his local association at the time the Bill was reaching its final stage in Parliament.

The Party prospects are as good as we could wish and when an election comes we may expect to overwhelm any opponent, or opponents, who may venture to come forward. I say this, though I am aware of very deep feeling and dissatisfaction on the part of many of our oldest supporters with the Government's India Policy. I have shared this feeling, but after careful consideration of the White Paper and more particularly of the Joint Committee's Report, and after hearing the debates on the Bill in the House of Commons, I have decided to support the Government's policy for these reasons:
1. I believe the new Government has a good prospect of success.
2. It does not mean getting out of India. We keep defence, foreign policy, and ecclesiastical matters, besides large measures of intervention and control.

3. The Indian people will work with us rather than against us . . . .
4. Matters have gone so far now that we cannot withdraw. The danger will be greater if we do than in case of future failure.
5. Self-government has for years been promised as our aim, and our word must be carried out. This is a step, and a big one.

Lastly, I should have urged that it is vital that our Party should not be divided. It is clear that a huge majority of the Party are in favour of the Government's policy. Let such as believe that the India policy must fail not break away from us, or fail to support us. For, if their fears are justified, we shall all be required to put matters straight. The Socialist policy is to give India absolute self-government and cut her adrift. If the Socialists win the next election, we lose not only India, but everything. It will be 1931 repeated, but worse.

East Grinstead Conservative Association, AGM Minutes, 16 March 1935.

document 23

The 'anti-appeasers' and the Munich crisis, 1938

The hesitancy and disunity of Neville Chamberlain's cirtics, which rendered their attacks ineffective, are illustrated by extracts from the diaries of one of their leaders, ex-Cabinet minister Leo Amery, and a backbencher, Anthony Crossley, at the height of the Czech crisis and the Munich conference.

Went to see Eden. I wanted to find out whether he was going to align himself with Churchill etc. and I wanted to prevent him taking precipitate action. I therefore told him that we had been invited to a conference by Winston in Lord Lloyd's house; that we had decided not to go; that we didn't wish to align ourselves with the Cabal who were notorious for plots against the Government.

Crossley diary, 20 September 1938 (**175**), part 3, p. 1170.

To Bracken's house in Lord North Street for a gathering of Winston's dissentients. The question was what attitude we should take on the Government motion. Winston and several others were all in favour of voting against the Government but I managed to persuade them that this was an unreasonable course unless they were ready to say that they had an alternative Government in sight.

I was prepared to go as far as abstaining which indicated disapproval of the particular policy but not a general hostility to the Government. That may be a weak line but I think one that can be defended in one's constituency. Anyhow it commended itself to the majority.

Amery diary, 5 October 1938 (**171**), p. 526.

document 24
The fall of Neville Chamberlain

The Norway debates of 7–8 May 1940 are eloquently described in the diary of a passionate supporter of Chamberlain, Henry 'Chips' Channon, Parliamentary Private Secretary to the junior Foreign Office minister R.A. Butler.

7 May 1940: A dreadful day: the political crisis overshadows everything: one cannot eat, sleep or concentrate. The 'glamour boys' are smacking their lips but their full strength is not yet known. I ran into the Prime Minister today in the House, and we chatted for a moment, but it was he who made the conversation, as I was suddenly stilled and made shy by my affection for him. Five minutes later he was speaking, and was given a warm welcome, but he spoke haltingly and did not make a good case: in fact he fumbled his words and seemed tired and embarrassed.... I realised at once the House was not with him ... the opening attack was a half-hearted affair, almost a failure.... The atmosphere was intense, and everywhere one heard whispers.

8 May 1940:... Feeling grew, still we thought we would survive. At last the Speaker called a division, which Winston nearly talked out. I went into the Aye Lobby, which seemed thin for a three line Whip, and we watched the insurgents file out of the Opposition Lobby (Teenie Cazalet could not make up his mind and abstained). 'Quislings', we shouted at them, 'Rats'. 'Yes-men', they replied. I saw all the expected ones, and many more – Hubert [Duggan] among them and my heart snapped against him for ever. Then I voted, as usual everyone wondered how many had dared to vote against us: so many threaten to do so, and funk it at the last moment.... [After the result] Neville appeared bowled over by the ominous figures, and was the first to rise. He looked grave and thoughtful and sad: as he walked calmly to the door, his supporters rose and cheered him lustily and he disappeared.

Channon diary, 7–8 May 1940 (**177**), pp. 244, 246–7.

document 25

The defeat of 1945

Sir Joseph Ball, Director of the Conservative Research Department 1930–39 and its Acting-Chairman 1943–45, analysed the causes of the 1945 election defeat in an internal Central Office memorandum written a few months afterwards.

In my opinion, we owe our defeat not to anything which happened during the election campaign itself, but to a persistent and ably-conducted campaign of Socialist propaganda which extended from the last General Election in November 1935 until July 1945, with no let-up whatever during the war.

We Conservatives (wrongly, I think) interpreted the political truce as barring us from all propaganda efforts. The Socialists, on the other hand, interpreted it as a by-election truce only, and both held and acted upon the view that they were entitled to conduct whatever propaganda they wished. It would require a good deal of investigation to assess the value of the various forms of Socialist propaganda, but there can be no doubt that the following all played their part:

(a) The regular publication of the Gollancz and other series of cheap books (*Guilty Men, Your M.P.*, etc.).

(b) The appointment of a prominent member of the Workers' Educational Association to direct the Army Bureau of Current Affairs, and the clever use made by the Socialists of many of the lectures. Many paid lecturers were Socialists, and made full use of their opportunities.

(c) The persistent use of the B.B.C. broadcasting service granted to prominent left-wing writers and politicians, and the left bias of many of the news reports and talks.

(d) Widespread newspaper propaganda in the columns of the left-wing national daily papers such as the *Daily Herald, Daily Mirror, News Chronicle, Daily Worker, The Star* . . .

(e) On top of this widespread press campaign, we had regular week-end speeches by leading Socialists, invariably well-reported not only by the press but also by the B.B.C., combined with clever use of the House of Commons debates for exploitation by left-wing newspapers.

(f) Finally, I have always thought that the publication, under Greenwood's authority, of the Beveridge Report before the cabinet had had an opportunity of considering it, was a clever propaganda move which played a great part in the Socialist campaign.

Memo by Ball, 'The next General Election', 1946, Conservative Party Archives, CCO/500/1/13.

document 26
Lord Woolton and the revival of the party organisation

After a business career and wartime office as Minister of Food, Lord Woolton served as a popular and successful Chairman of the Party from 1946 to 1955. He recalls the structure which he found, and some of his responses.

The organization of the Conservative Party was the most topsy-like arrangement that I had ever come across. It had grown up amidst conflicting and – it seemed – almost irreconcilable claims.... I faced up to the fact that whilst as Chairman of the Party I had received an enthusiastic welcome from the associations, I had, on paper, no control over their activities: they selected their candidates; they selected their agent, and employed him; they arranged their meetings, and were at liberty to make direct approach to any speakers they desired. I depended on their goodwill, which obviously they were anxious to give, in the creation of a headquarters staff that would be so efficient in performance and so approachable in manner, that their influence would overcome their lack of authority; I relied on the Central Office earning the goodwill and the confidence of all these diversified bodies which troubled my business instincts; if we could do that, I knew that we should, in the end, find them coming of their own free will into one common organization....

I rejected caution and decided to ask for a fund of one million pounds, thereby demonstrating my faith in the willingness of the Party to make sacrifices in order to convince the electors of the country of the rightness of the Conservative approach. These were shock tactics.... This bold demand created an infectious and compelling enthusiasm. People went out for this apparently unassailable goal, and the stimulation of this widespread effort among all the grades of society of which the Conservative Party is composed not only produced the million pounds that I had asked for, but it gave the Party a sense of accomplishment. Their hopes revived; they found that people believed in them in spite of the recent · electoral defeat; they recruited members and workers. . . .

It is always dangerous in politics to be committed to detail in any programme. But I concluded that it was at least as dangerous to be so vague that the nation could think that the Conservatism that we were expounding would be no different from the Conservatism of the 'thirties. We therefore decided to take the risk of defining in terms the policies we would encourage the nation to undertake.

Lord Woolton, *The Memoirs of the Rt Hon. the Earl of Woolton*, Cassell, 1959, pp. 331, 336–7, 347.

document 27

The Industrial Charter

The most important of the policy documents produced in opposition was The Industrial Charter, *published in May 1947. The work of the Industrial Policy Committee, chaired by R.A. Butler, it was endorsed by Churchill despite his reservations. In fact it was significant as a symbolic gesture rather than as a programme of action; however, the optimism which it expresses is strikingly different in tone from* **doc. 1**.

Man cannot live by economics alone. Human nature will give of its best only when inspired by a sense of confidence and hope. We base all our plans on a belief in the unlimited power of the human personality to meet and to overcome difficulties and to rise above them. We are completely opposed to the imposition of a rigid strait-jacket of doctrinaire political theory, either upon the individual regardless of his individuality or upon the nation regardless of the economic facts of the moment. Our abiding objective is to free industry from unnecessary controls and restrictions. We wish to substitute for the present paralysis, in which we are experiencing the worst of all worlds, a system of free enterprise, which is on terms with authority, and which reconciles the need for central direction with the encouragement of individual effort. We point to a way of life designed to free private endeavour from the taunt of selfishness or self-interest and public control from the reproach of meddlesome interference. . . .

The desire for increased rewards, whether it be expressed in terms of the profit motive or higher wages, animates the great bulk of mankind. We hold that there should be healthy rewards for work done. We shall propose methods to curb monopolies and unfair privileges. We are determined to restore by all reasonable means that great stimulus to personal endeavour – fair incentive. A restoration of freedom and incentives would not mean, as has been falsely held, an end to security in our social and industrial system. Justice demands that the aim of national policy should be to provide a basic standard of living and security of outlook for all our people. This can be achieved in a variety of ways. Our national system of social services, which we have helped to create, has recently been enlarged to cover better provision for pensioners in their old age, for the sick through the universal health service, for the unemployed, for widows and for parents of large families. But something more than provision for exceptional circumstances is necessary. . . . We describe how each individual must be given the chance to rise above the level of security and to win special rewards. Justice is frustrated by exact equality of reward to all, but it is found where there is equality of opportunity and incentive to win a variety of rewards.

The Industrial Charter, May 1947, pp. 3–4.

Appendix 1 Leaders and Office-holders

Leader of the Party		*Appointed*
Arthur Balfour		14 July 1902
Andrew Bonar Law	(Leader in the House of Commons only)	13 Nov. 1911
Austen Chamberlain	(Leader in the House of Commons only)	21 Mar. 1921
Andrew Bonar Law		23 Oct. 1922
Stanley Baldwin		28 May 1923
Neville Chamberlain		31 May 1937
Winston Churchill		9 Oct. 1940

Leader of the Party in the House of Lords

8th Duke of Devonshire	12 July 1902
5th Marquess of Lansdowne	13 Oct. 1903
1st Earl Curzon (elevated to 1st Marquess, 1921)	10 Dec. 1916
4th Marquess of Salisbury	27 Apr. 1925
1st Viscount Hailsham	17 June 1931
7th Marquess of Londonderry	7 June 1935
3rd Viscount Halifax	22 Nov. 1935
7th Earl Stanhope	9 Mar. 1938
1st Viscount Caldecote	14 May 1940
3rd Viscount Halifax	3 Oct. 1940
1st Baron Lloyd	10 Jan. 1941
1st Baron Moyne	8 Feb. 1941
Viscount Cranborne (5th Marquess of Salisbury, 1947)	22 Feb. 1942

Chief Whip in the House of Commons

Sir William Walrond	29 June 1895
Sir Alexander Acland-Hood	8 Aug. 1902
Lord Balcarres (courtesy title, son of Earl of Crawford)	1 July 1911

Appendix 1

Lord Edmund Talbot (courtesy title, son of Duke of Norfolk)	4 Feb. 1913
Leslie Wilson	1 Apr. 1921
Bolton Eyres-Monsell	25 July 1923
David Margesson	10 Nov. 1931
James Stuart	14 Jan. 1941
Patrick Buchan-Hepburn	4 July 1948

Chairman of the Party Organisation

Arthur Steel-Maitland	26 June 1911
Sir George Younger	1 Jan. 1917
Francis Stanley Jackson	13 Mar. 1923
John Colin Campbell Davidson	4 Nov. 1926
Neville Chamberlain	23 June 1930
1st Baron Stonehaven	14 Apr. 1931
Douglas Hacking (created Baronet, 1938)	2 Mar. 1936
Thomas Dugdale	6 Mar. 1942
Ralph Assheton	29 Oct. 1944
1st Baron Woolton (elevated to 1st Viscount, 1953)	1 July 1946

Professional head of the Central Office organisation

Robert Middleton	Principal Agent	July 1885
Lionel Wells	"	July 1903
Alexander Haig	"	Nov. 1905
Percival Hughes	"	Dec. 1906
John Boraston	"{ Joint June 1915–Apr. 1920	May 1912
William Jenkins	"{ Joint June 1915–Apr. 1920	June 1915
Sir Malcolm Fraser	"	Dec. 1920
Sir Reginald Hall	"	Mar. 1923
Herbert Blain	"	Mar. 1924
Sir T.J. Leigh Maclachlan	"	Jan. 1927
H. Robert Topping	" (General Director, Feb. 1931–)	Feb. 1928
Stephen Pierssene	General Director	Oct. 1945

Appendix 2 Conservative Performance in General Elections

Before 1918 constituencies polled on different days, and the date shown for the general elections of 1900–10 is that of the first polls: with the exception of Orkney & Shetlands and the university seats, the remaining seats polled in the course of the following 14–16 days. In the 1918 and 1945 elections the count was delayed until 28 December and 26 July, respectively, to allow for the collection of the postal ballots from the forces overseas.

The figures for 1900–10 include Liberal Unionists; those for 1931 and 1935 do *not* include other groups in the National Government, but the remaining Nationals and National Liberals are included in figures for 1945–51.

Date of election	Candidates nominated	Unopposed returns	MPs elected	Total votes received	% Share of vote
1 Oct. 1900	569	163	402	1,767,958	50.3
12 Jan. 1906	556	13	156	2,422,071	43.4
15 Jan. 1910	594	19	272	3,104,407	46.8
3 Dec. 1910	548	72	272	2,420,169	46.6
14 Dec. 1918	445	41	382	4,144,192	38.6
15 Nov. 1922	482	42	344	5,502,298	38.5
6 Dec. 1923	536	35	258	5,514,541	38.0
29 Oct. 1924	534	16	412	7,854,523	46.8
30 May 1929	590	4	260	8,656,225	38.1
27 Oct. 1931	518	49	470	11,905,925	55.0
14 Nov. 1935	515	23	387	10,496,300	47.8
5 July 1945	618	1	210	9,972,010	39.6
23 Feb. 1950	619	2	298	12,492,404	43.5
25 Oct. 1951	617	4	321	13,718,199	48.0

Bibliography

THE CONSERVATIVE PARTY: GENERAL SURVEYS
1   Blake, R., *The Conservative Party from Peel to Churchill*, Eyre & Spottiswoode, 1970; extended edition, Methuen, 1985.
2   Butler, Lord, ed., *The Conservatives: A History from their Origins to 1965*, Allen & Unwin, 1977.
3   Lindsay, T.F. and Harrington, M., *The Conservative Party 1918–79*, Macmillan, 1979.
4   Norton, P. and Aughey, A., *Conservatives and Conservatism*, Temple Smith, 1981.
5   Pugh, M., 'Popular Conservatism in Britain: Continuity and Change 1880–1987', *Journal of British Studies*, xxvii, 1988.
6   Ramsden, J.A., *The Age of Balfour and Baldwin 1902–40*, Longman, 1978.
7   Seldon, A. and Ball, S., eds, *Conservative Century: The Conservative Party since 1900*, Oxford University Press, 1994.
8   Southgate, D., ed., *The Conservative Leadership 1832–1932*, Macmillan, 1974.

THE EVOLUTION OF THE CONSERVATIVE PARTY, 1832–1902
9   Close, D., 'The Rise of the Conservatives in the Age of Reform', *Bulletin of the Institute of Historical Research*, xlv, 1972.
10 Coleman, B., *Conservatism and the Conservative Party in Nineteenth-Century Britain*, Edward Arnold, 1988.
11 Cornford, J.P., 'The Transformation of Conservatism in the Late Nineteenth Century', *Victorian Studies*, vii, 1963–64.
12 Feuchtwanger, E.J., *Disraeli, Democracy and the Tory Party*, Oxford University Press, 1968.
13 Fraser, P., 'The Liberal Unionist Alliance: Chamberlain, Hartington, and the Conservatives 1886–1904', *English Historical Review*, lxxvii, 1962.
14 Marsh, P., *The Discipline of Popular Government: Lord Salisbury's Domestic Statecraft 1881–1902*, Harvester, 1978.

15 Newbould, I., 'Sir Robert Peel and the Conservative Party 1832–41', *English Historical Review*, xcviii, 1983.

16 Shannon, R., *The Age of Disraeli 1867–81: The Rise of Tory Democracy*, Longman, 1992.

17 Stewart, R., *The Foundation of the Conservative Party 1832–67*, Longman, 1978.

THE PARTY LEADERSHIP, 1902–51

18 Addison, P., *Churchill on the Home Front 1900–55*, Cape, 1992.

19 Amery, J., *Joseph Chamberlain and the Tariff Reform Campaign: The Life of Joseph Chamberlain*, vols. 5 and 6, Macmillan, 1969.

20 Blake, R., *The Unknown Prime Minister: The Life and Times of Andrew Bonar Law*, Eyre & Spottiswoode, 1955.

21 Blake, R. and Louis, W.R., eds, *Churchill*, Oxford University Press, 1993.

22 Campbell, J., *F.E. Smith, 1st Earl of Birkenhead*, Cape, 1983.

23 Charmley, J., *Duff Cooper*, Weidenfeld & Nicolson, 1986.

24 Charmley, J., *Churchill: The End of Glory*, Hodder & Stoughton, 1993.

25 Chilston, Lord, *Chief Whip: The Political Life and Times of Aretas Akers-Douglas, 1st Viscount Chilston*, Routledge, 1961.

26 Churchill, R., *Lord Derby: King of Lancashire*, Heinemann, 1959.

27 Cross, J.A., *Sir Samuel Hoare*, Cape, 1977.

28 Cross, J.A., *Lord Swinton*, Oxford University Press, 1982.

29 Dilks, D., *Neville Chamberlain*, vol. 1, *1869–1929*, Cambridge University Press, 1984; the first volume of a new official biography.

30 Dutton, D., *Austen Chamberlain*, Ross Anderson, 1985.

31 Egremont, M., *Balfour*, Collins, 1980.

32 Gilbert, M., *Churchill: A Life*, Heinemann, 1991; single-volume summation of the 8-volume official biography.

33 Gollin, A.M., *Proconsul in Politics: A Study of Lord Milner in Opposition and in Power*, Anthony Blond, 1964.

34 Horne, A., *Macmillan*, vol. 1, *1894–1956*, Macmillan, 1988.

35 Howard, A., *Rab: The Life of R.A. Butler*, Cape, 1987.

36 Hyde, H.M., *Baldwin*, Hart-Davis & MacGibbon, 1973.

37 James, R.R., *Churchill: A Study in Failure 1900–39*, Weidenfeld & Nicolson, 1970.

38 James, R.R., *Anthony Eden*, Weidenfeld & Nicolson, 1986.

39 Jay, R., *Joseph Chamberlain*, Oxford University Press, 1981.

40   Jenkins, R., *Baldwin*, Collins, 1987.

41   Judd, D., *Radical Joe: A Life of Joseph Chamberlain*, Hamish Hamilton, 1977.

42   Mackay, R.F., *Balfour: Intellectual Statesman*, Oxford University Press, 1985.

43   Mackintosh, J.P., ed., *British Prime Ministers in the 20th Century*, vol. 1, Weidenfeld & Nicolson, 1977.

44   Macleod, I., *Neville Chamberlain*, Muller, 1961.

45   Middlemas, K. and Barnes, J., *Baldwin – A Biography*, Weidenfeld & Nicolson, 1969.

46   Morris, M., '"Et l'honneur?": Politics and Principles – A Case Study of Austen Chamberlain', in Wrigley, C., ed., *Warfare, Diplomacy and Politics*, Hamish Hamilton, 1986.

47   O'Brien, T., *Milner*, Constable, 1979.

48   Pelling, H., *Winston Churchill*, Macmillan, 1974.

49   Roberts, A., *The Holy Fox: A Biography of Lord Halifax*, Weidenfeld, 1991.

THE PARLIAMENTARY PARTY, 1902–51

50   Ball, S., 'The 1922 Committee: The Formative Years 1922–45', *Parliamentary History*, ix, 1990.

51   Ball, S., 'Parliament and Politics in Britain 1900–51', *Parliamentary History*, x, 1991.

52   Close, D.H., 'The Growth of Backbench Organisation in the Conservative Party', *Parliamentary Affairs*, xxvii, 1974.

53   Cornford, J., 'The Parliamentary Foundations of the "Hotel Cecil"', in Robson, R., ed., *Ideas and Institutions of Victorian Britain*, Bell, 1967.

54   Cross, J.A., 'The Withdrawal of the Conservative Party Whip', *Parliamentary Affairs*, xxi, 1967–68.

55   Goodhart, P. and Branston, U., *The 1922: The Story of the Conservative Backbenchers Parliamentary Committee*, Macmillan, 1973.

56   McEwen, J.M., 'The Coupon Election of 1918 and Unionist Members of Parliament', *Journal of Modern History*, xxxiv, 1962.

57   Moore, S., 'The Agrarian Conservative Party in Parliament 1920–29', *Parliamentary History*, x, 1991.

58   Rempel, R.A., 'Lord Hugh Cecil's Parliamentary Career 1900–14: Promise Unfulfilled', *Journal of British Studies*, xi, 1972.

THE PARTY ORGANISATION, 1902–51

59 Beichman, A., 'Hugger-Mugger in Old Queen Street: The Origins of the Conservative Research Department', *Journal of Contemporary History*, xiii, 1978.

60 Fawcett, A., *Conservative Agent: A Study of the National Society of Conservative and Unionist Agents and its Members*, National Society of Conservative Agents, 1967.

61 Hollins, T.J., 'The Conservative Party and Film Propaganda between the Wars', *English Historical Review*, 96, 1981.

62 Jones, R.B., 'Balfour's Reforms of Party Organisation', *Bulletin of the Institute of Historical Research*, xxxviii, 1965.

63 Layton-Henry, Z., 'The Young Conservatives 1945–70', *Journal of Contemporary History*, viii, 1973.

64 McKenzie, R.T., *British Political Parties*, Heinemann, 1955.

65 Pugh, M., *The Tories and the People 1880–1935*, Blackwell, 1985.

66 Ramsden, J.A., *The Making of Conservative Party Policy: The Conservative Research Department since 1929*, Longman, 1980.

67 Ramsden, J.A., 'Baldwin and Film', in Pronay, N. and Spring, D.W., eds, *Politics, Propaganda and Film 1918–45*, Macmillan, 1982.

68 Robb, J., *The Primrose League 1883–1906*, Columbia University Press, 1942.

69 Urwin, D.W., 'The Development of the Conservative Party Organisation in Scotland until 1912', *Scottish Historical Review*, xliv, 1965.

CONSERVATISM: PRINCIPLES AND POLICIES

70 Addison, P., 'The Political Beliefs of Winston Churchill', *Royal Historical Society, Transactions*, 5th Series, xxx, 1980.

71 Cain, P., 'Political Economy in Edwardian England: The Tariff Reform Controversy', in O'Day, A., ed., *The Edwardian Age 1900–14*, Macmillan, 1979.

72 Cunningham, H., 'The Conservative Party and Patriotism', in Colls, R. and Dodd, P., eds, *Englishness: Politics and Culture 1880–1920*, Croom Helm, 1986.

73 Dean, D.W., 'Conservatism and the National Education System 1922–40', *Journal of Contemporary History*, vi, 1971.

74 Eccleshall, R., ed., *English Conservatism since the Restoration*, Unwin Hyman, 1990.

75 Fair, J.D. and Hutcheson, J.A., 'British Conservatism in the

Twentieth Century: An Emerging Ideological Tradition', *Albion*, xix, 1987.

76 Fforde, M., *Conservatism and Collectivism 1880–1914*, Edinburgh University Press, 1990.

77 Glickman, H., 'The Toryness of English Conservatism', *Journal of British Studies*, i, 1961.

78 Greenaway, J., 'British Conservatism and Bureaucracy', *History of Political Thought*, xiii, 1992.

79 O'Gorman, F., ed., *British Conservatism: Conservative Thought from Burke to Thatcher*, Longman, 1986.

80 Rodner, W.S., 'Conservatism, Resistance and Lord Hugh Cecil', *History of Political Thought*, ix, 1988.

81 Thompson, J.A. and Mejia, A., eds, *Edwardian Conservatism: Five Studies in Adaptation*, Croom Helm, 1988.

82 Webber, G.C., *The Ideology of the British Right 1918–39*, Croom Helm, 1986.

83 Williams, R., *Defending the Empire: The Conservative Party and British Defence Policy 1899–1915*, Yale University Press, 1991.

84 Williamson, P., 'The Doctrinal Politics of Stanley Baldwin', in Bentley, M., ed., *Public and Private Doctrine*, Cambridge University Press, 1993.

THE EDWARDIAN CRISIS, 1902–14

85 Blewett, N., 'Free-Fooders, Balfourites, and Whole-Hoggers: Factionalism within the Unionist Party 1906–10', *Historical Journal*, xi, 1968.

86 Blewett, N., *The Peers, the Parties, and the People: The General Elections of 1910*, Macmillan, 1972.

87 Coetzee, F., *For Party or Country: Nationalism and the Dilemmas of Popular Conservatism in Edwardian England*, Oxford University Press, 1990.

88 Dutton, D., 'Unionist Politics and the Aftermath of the General Election of 1906: A Reassessment', *Historical Journal*, xxii, 1979.

89 Dutton, D., 'The Unionist Party and Social Policy 1906–14', *Historical Journal*, xxiv, 1981.

90 Dutton, D., *His Majesty's Loyal Opposition: The Unionist Party in Opposition 1905–15*, Liverpool University Press, 1992.

91 Fanning, R., 'The Unionist Party and Ireland 1906–10', *Irish Historical Studies*, xv, 1966–67.

92 Fanning, R., '"Rats" versus "Ditchers": The Diehard Revolt and the Parliament Bill of 1911', in Cosgrove, A. and McGuire, J., eds, *Parliament and Community*, Appletree Press, 1983.

93   Fraser, P., 'Unionism and Tariff Reform: The Crisis of 1906', *Historical Journal*, v, 1962.

94   Fraser, P., 'The Unionist Débâcle of 1911 and Balfour's Retirement', *Journal of Modern History*, xxxv, 1963.

95   Gollin, A.M., *Balfour's Burden: Arthur Balfour and Imperial Preference*, Anthony Blond, 1965; a detailed account of the Cabinet splits of 1903.

96   Green, E.H.H., 'Radical Conservatism: The Electoral Genesis of Tariff Reform', *Historical Journal*, xxviii, 1985.

97   McCready, H.W., 'The Revolt of the Unionist Free Traders', *Parliamentary Affairs*, xvi, 1963.

98   Marrison, A.J., 'Businessmen, Industries, and Tariff Reform in Great Britain 1903–30', *Business History*, xxviii, 1983.

99   Murphy, R., 'Faction in the Conservative Party and the Home Rule Crisis 1912–14', *History*, lxxi, 1986.

100 Murray, B.K., *The People's Budget 1909–10*, Oxford University Press, 1980.

101 Phillips, G.D., *The Diehards: Aristocratic Society and Politics in Edwardian England*, Harvard University Press, 1979.

102 Phillips, G.D., 'Lord Willoughby de Broke and the Politics of Radical Toryism 1909–14', *Journal of British Studies*, xx, 1981.

103 Rempel, R.A., *Unionists Divided: Arthur Balfour, Joseph Chamberlain, and the Unionist Free Traders*, David & Charles, 1972.

104 Ridley, J., 'The Unionist Social Reform Committee 1911–14: Wets before the Deluge', *Historical Journal*, xxx, 1987.

105 Ridley, J., 'The Unionist Opposition and the House of Lords 1906–10', *Parliamentary History*, xi, 1992.

106 Rodner, W.S., 'Leaguers, Covenanters, Moderates: British Support for Ulster 1913–14', *Eire-Ireland*, xvii, 1982.

107 Russell, A.K., *Liberal Landslide: The General Election of 1906*, David & Charles, 1973.

108 Searle, G.R., 'Critics of Edwardian Society: The Case of the Radical Right', in O'Day, A., ed., *The Edwardian Age 1900–14*, Macmillan, 1979.

109 Southern, D., 'Lord Newton, the Conservative Peers, and the Parliament Act of 1911', *English Historical Review*, xcvi, 1981.

110 Smith, J., 'Bluff, Bluster and Brinkmanship: Andrew Bonar

Law and the Third Home Rule Bill', *Historical Journal*, xxxvi, 1993.

111 Stewart, A.T.Q., *The Ulster Crisis: Resistance to Home Rule 1912–14*, Faber, 1967.

112 Sykes, A., 'The Confederacy and the Purge of the Unionist Free Traders 1906–10', *Historical Journal*, xviii, 1975.

113 Sykes, A., *Tariff Reform in British Politics 1903–13*, Oxford University Press, 1979.

114 Sykes, A., 'The Radical Right and the Crisis of Conservatism before the First World War', *Historical Journal*, xxvi, 1983.

115 Weston, C.C. and Kelvin, P., 'The "Judas Group" and the Parliament Bill of 1911', *English Historical Review*, xcix, 1984.

116 Zebel, S.H., 'Joseph Chamberlain and the Genesis of Tariff Reform', *Journal of British Studies*, vii, 1967.

WAR AND COALITION, 1914–22

117 Close, D.H., 'Conservatives and Coalition after the First World War', *Journal of Modern History*, xlv, 1973.

118 Cowling, M., *The Impact of Labour 1920–24: The Beginning of Modern British Politics*, Cambridge University Press, 1971.

119 Cuthbert, D.D., 'Lloyd George and the Conservative Central Office 1918–22', in Taylor, A.J.P., ed., *Lloyd George: Twelve Essays*, Hamish Hamilton, 1971.

120 Hazlehurst, C., *Politicians at War: July 1914 to May 1915*, Cape, 1971.

121 Kinnear, M., *The Fall of Lloyd George: The Political Crisis of 1922*, Macmillan, 1973.

122 Morgan, K.O., *Consensus and Disunity: The Lloyd George Coalition Government 1918–22*, Oxford University Press, 1979.

123 Murphy, R., 'Walter Long, the Unionist Ministers, and the Formation of Lloyd George's Government in December 1916', *Historical Journal*, xxix, 1986.

124 Pugh, M., 'Asquith, Bonar Law, and the First Coalition', *Historical Journal*, xvii, 1974.

125 Ramsden, J., 'The Newport By-election and the Fall of the Coalition', in Cook, C. and Ramsden, J., eds, *By-elections in British Politics*, Macmillan, 1973.

126 Rubinstein, W.D., 'Henry Page Croft and the National Party 1917–22', *Journal of Contemporary History*, ix, 1974.

127 Stubbs, J., 'The Impact of the Great War on the Conservative Party', in Peele, G. and Cook, C., eds, *The Politics of Reappraisal 1918–39*, Macmillan, 1975.

128 Stubbs, J., 'The Unionists and Ireland 1914–18', *Historical Journal*, xxxiii, 1990.

129 Turner, J., *British Politics and the Great War: Coalition and Conflict 1915–18*, Yale University Press, 1992.

THE AGE OF BALDWIN, 1922–39

130 Ball, S., 'Failure of an Opposition? The Conservative Party in Parliament 1929–31', *Parliamentary History*, v, 1986.

131 Ball, S., 'The Conservative Party and the Formation of the National Government: August 1931', *Historical Journal*, xxix, 1986.

132 Ball, S., *Baldwin and the Conservative Party: The Crisis of 1929–31*, Yale University Press, 1988.

133 Ball, S., 'The Politics of Appeasement: The Fall of the Duchess of Atholl and the Kinross & West Perth By-election, December 1938', *Scottish Historical Review*, lxix, 1990.

134 Ball, S., 'The Conservative Dominance 1918–40', *Modern History Review*, iii, 1991.

135 Bridge, C., 'Conservatism and Indian Reform 1929–39', *Journal of Imperial and Commonwealth History*, iv, 1975–76.

136 Bridge, C., 'Churchill, Hoare, Derby, and the Committee of Privileges: April to June 1934', *Historical Journal*, xxii, 1979.

137 Bridge, C., *Holding India to the Empire: the British Conservative Party and the 1935 Constitution*, Sterling, 1986.

138 Close, D.H., 'The Collapse of Resistance to Democracy: Conservatives, Adult Suffrage, and Second Chamber Reform 1911–28', *Historical Journal*, xx, 1977.

139 Coleman, B., 'The Conservative Party and the Frustration of the Extreme Right', in Thorpe, A., ed., *The Failure of Political Extremism in Inter-war Britain*, University of Exeter Press, 1989.

140 Cook, C., *The Age of Alignment: Electoral Politics in Britain 1922–29*, Macmillan, 1975.

141 Cowling, M., *The Impact of Hitler: British Politics and British Policy 1933–40*, Cambridge University Press, 1975.

142 Fair, J.D., 'The Conservative Basis for the Formation of the National Government of 1931', *Journal of British Studies*, xix, 1980.

143 Hazlehurst, C., 'The Baldwinite Conspiracy', *Historical Studies*, xvi, 1974–75.

144 McCrillis, N.R., 'Taming Democracy? The Conservative Party and House of Lords' Reform 1916–29', *Parliamentary History*, xii, 1993.

145 McKibbin, R., 'Class and Conventional Wisdom: The Conservative Party and the "Public" in Inter-war Britain', in McKibbin, R., *The Ideologies of Class*, Oxford University Press, 1990.

146 Peele, G., 'St George's and the Empire Crusade', in Cook, C. and Ramsden, J., eds, *By-elections in British Politics*, Macmillan, 1973.

147 Peele, G., 'Revolt over India', in Peele, G. and Cook, C., eds, *The Politics of Reappraisal 1918–39*, Macmillan, 1975.

148 Rasmussen, J.S., 'Government and Intra-Party Opposition: Dissent within the Conservative Parliamentary Party in the 1930s', *Political Studies*, xix, 1971.

149 Schinness, R., 'The Conservative Party and Anglo-Soviet Relations 1925–27', *European Studies Review*, vii, 1977.

150 Self, R., 'Conservative Reunion and the General Election of 1923: A Reassessment', *Twentieth Century British History*, iii, 1992.

151 Stannage, T., *Baldwin Thwarts the Opposition: The British General Election of 1935*, Croom Helm, 1980.

152 Thompson, N., *The Anti-Appeasers: Conservative Opposition to Appeasement in the 1930s*, Oxford University Press, 1971.

153 Thorpe, A., *The British General Election of 1931*, Oxford University Press, 1991.

154 Williamson, P., '"Safety First": Baldwin, the Conservative Party, and the 1929 General Election', *Historical Journal*, xxv, 1982.

155 Williamson, P., *National Crisis and National Government: British Politics, the Economy and Empire 1926–32*, Cambridge University Press, 1992.

156 Wrench, D.J., 'Cashing In: The Parties and the National Government, August 1931–September 1932', *Journal of British Studies*, xxiii, 1984.

DISASTER AND RECOVERY, 1939–51

157 Addison, P., *The Road to 1945: British Politics and the Second World War*, Cape, 1975.

158 Dilks, D., 'The Twilight War and the Fall of France: Chamberlain and Churchill in 1940', in Dilks, D., ed., *Retreat from Power*, vol. 2, Macmillan, 1981.

159 Fair, J.D., 'The Norwegian Campaign and Winston Churchill's Rise to Power in 1940', *International History Review*, ix, 1987.

160 Harris, N., *Competition and the Corporate Society: British Conservatives, the State and Industry 1945–64*, Methuen, 1972.

161 Hoffman, J.D., *The Conservative Party in Opposition 1945–51*, MacGibbon & Kee, 1964.

162 Jefferys, K., 'May 1940: The Downfall of Neville Chamberlain', *Parliamentary History*, x, 1991.

163 Jefferys, K., *The Churchill Coalition and Wartime Politics 1940–45*, Manchester University Press, 1991.

164 Lee, J.M., *The Churchill Coalition*, Batsford, 1980.

165 Ramsden, J., '"A Party for Owners or a Party for Earners": How Far Did the British Conservative Party Really Change after 1945?', *Royal Historical Society, Transactions*, 5th series, xxxvii, 1987.

166 Ramsden, J., 'Conservatives since 1945', *Contemporary Record*, ii, 1988.

167 Rasmussen, J.S., 'Party Discipline in Wartime: The Downfall of the Chamberlain Government', *Journal of Politics*, xxxii, 1970.

168 Schwarz, B., 'The Tide of History: The Reconstruction of Conservatism 1945–51', in Tiratsoo, N., ed., *The Attlee Years*, Pinter, 1991.

DOCUMENTARY SOURCES

169 Ball, S., ed., *Parliament and Politics in the Age of Baldwin and MacDonald: The Headlam Diary 1923–35*, Historians' Press, 1992.

170 Barnes, J. and Nicholson, D., eds, *The Leo Amery Diaries*, vol. 1, *1899–1929*, Hutchinson, 1980.

171 Barnes, J. and Nicholson, D., eds, *The Empire at Bay – The Leo Amery Diaries*, vol. 2, *1929–45*, Hutchinson, 1988.

172 Boyce, D.G., ed., *The Crisis of British Unionism: The Domestic Political Papers of the 2nd Earl of Selborne 1885–1922*, Historians' Press, 1987.

173 Chamberlain, A., *Politics from Inside: An Epistolatory Chronicle 1906–14*, Cassell, 1936.

174 Cockett, R.B., ed., *My dear Max: The Letters of Brendan Bracken to Lord Beaverbrook 1925–58*, Historians' Press, 1990.

175 Gilbert, M., ed., *Winston S. Churchill*, vol. V, *Companion Documents*, 3 parts, Heinemann, 1979, 1981, 1982.

176 James, R.R., ed., *Memoirs of a Conservative: J.C.C. Davidson's Memoirs and Papers 1910–37*, Weidenfeld & Nicolson, 1969.

177 James, R.R., ed., *Chips: The Diaries of Sir Henry Channon,* Weidenfeld & Nicolson, 1967.

178 Jones, T., *A Diary with Letters 1931–50,* Oxford University Press, 1954.

179 Ramsden, J.A., ed., *Real Old Tory Politics: The Political Diaries of Sir Robert Sanders, Lord Bayford: 1910–35,* Historians' Press, 1984.

180 Ridley, J. and Percy, C., eds, *The Letters of Arthur Balfour and Lady Elcho 1885–1917,* Hamish Hamilton, 1992.

181 Vincent, J., ed., *The Crawford Papers,* Manchester University Press, 1984.

182 Williamson, P., ed., *The Modernisation of Conservative Politics: The Diaries and Letters of William Bridgeman 1904–35,* Historians' Press, 1988.

Index